"Larry Taylor has taught his Kingdom Family class for the past thirteen years to hundreds of our church and school families at Prestonwood. I have personally witnessed the impact on families and parents from Larry's training and practical applications of biblical principles. Parents are encouraged and are embracing their role in the discipleship of their children. This is a must-read for all parents! We can and we must train our children to run with the horses!"

—Dr. Jack Graham, *Pastor, Prestonwood Church*

"My friendship with Larry Taylor and our work together with students, parents and educators has allowed me to see his heart for the family. Larry's concepts and practical application conveyed in this book are consistent with both biblical principles and parenting best practices. This is a must-read for parents and professionals who are training our children—the next generation."

—Josh McDowell, *Josh McDowell Ministries, Christian apologist and author*

"As President and Founder of Student Leadership University, I've spent my life trying to remind parents and students that, 'the future belongs to those who are prepared.' I am very excited that my friend and one of the leading players in education, Larry Taylor, has written *Running with the Horses*. This book is a must-read for every parent and teacher. It is one of the most effective and motivational sets of instructions I've seen to help you equip your most cherished possessions to not only be able to run in this culture but also to stand tall and soar like an eagle. I'm going to do all that I can to make sure it gets in the hands of parents."

—Dr. Jay Strack, *President and Founder of Student Leadership University*

"Some authors should be read because they really know their stuff. Some authors should be read because they've lived it out. There are a few authors, like Larry Taylor, who qualify on both counts. I've admired Larry's leadership in Christian education, and witnessed firsthand how he has implemented what he's written about in this book. And, I know he's done it as a dad, too, while leading hundreds of families to do the same through his teaching and training efforts. I'm thrilled that his wisdom will get to a broader audience through this book."

—John Stonestreet, *Summit Ministries and Colson Center for Christian Worldview; speaker, writer, cultural commentator, and collaborator of worldview initiatives*

"In a world where the deterioration of the moral fabric of the family unit is so prevalent, Larry Taylor's book, *Running with the Horses* provides practical training that equips parents with real life application to maximize the success of growing Godly character leaders. It is full of biblically based relevance that inspires and nurtures intentional parenting. A must-read for any parent that desires to raise their children to be the full expression that God created them to be."

—Linda Paulk, CEO, *Sky Ranch Ministries*

"We are humbled and grateful to call Larry Taylor our dad. He is—we can attest—a man of great wisdom, courage and integrity, and we hope that other Christian parents will find in this book not only practical advice, but also inspiration and encouragement."

—Bryce, Luke, Zeke and Chas Taylor *(sons of author Larry Taylor)*

Running with the Horses

A Parenting Guide for Raising Children to be Servant-Leaders for Christ

LARRY TAYLOR, Ph.D.

WESTBOW
PRESS
A DIVISION OF THOMAS NELSON

WestBow Press books may be ordered through booksellers or by contacting:

WestBow Press
A Division of Thomas Nelson
1663 Liberty Drive
Bloomington, IN 47403
www.westbowpress.com
1-(866) 928-1240

ISBN: 978-1-4908-0851-2 (sc)
ISBN: 978-1-4908-0852-9 (hc)
ISBN: 978-1-4908-0850-5 (e)

Library of Congress Control Number: 2013916724

Printed in the United States of America.

WestBow Press rev. date: 10/14/2013

I dedicate this book to my wife, Delinda Rose, and to our four sons, Bryce, Luke, Zeke, and Chas.

Table of Contents

Introduction

We all have great intentions when it comes to raising our children. We want them to succeed, to experience joy, and above all, to surrender their lives to the Lordship of Christ. As a father of four boys and a twenty-five-year veteran of school administration, I understand these goals. I also understand the busyness of daily life, how days merge into weeks as our hurried lifestyles spin out of control, leaving us wondering how our toddlers became teenagers. It is admirable to want our children to succeed. It is scriptural to have a deliberate plan to make this dream a reality. That is what this book is all about: introducing you to a simple, biblically-based plan for raising servant-leaders for Christ.

Throughout this book you will be presented with compelling new research suggesting that the traditional training methods used to teach our children are good but incomplete. The ethos of our culture isn't Christian anymore, and for the most part, our kids are entering a culture opposed to absolute truth, opposed to the tenets of Christianity, opposed to living a life of holiness.

An alarming study recently conducted by the Barna Group, 2007-2011, (Faith that Lasts Project) revealed that "about three out of ten young people who grow up with a Christian background stay faithful to church and to faith throughout their transitions from the teen years through their twenties."

Why is this mass exodus occurring? I believe it is because our children and students are woefully unprepared. We are sending them into the game of life armed with snippets of

Scripture and a vague understanding of their commitment to God.

It is my belief that, in order to counteract our culture's impact on our children and to produce biblically literate and confident disciples of Christ, we need only to look to Jesus' own training method. His plan was defined, deliberate, and deep. He understood the task ahead of Him, He created situations to produce depth in His followers' belief system, and He was deliberate—using common, relevant examples to permanently engrave His teachings upon their hearts. These three principles established by Christ should serve as the foundation for raising our children. And, as you continue to read *Running with the Horses*, you will see that the book has specific sections devoted to these three areas: Defining the Race, Creating a Deliberate Plan, and Developing Depth.

The theme for this book is, "If you have run with footmen and they have tired you out, then how can you compete with horses? If you fall down in a land of peace, how will you do in the thicket of the Jordan?" (Jeremiah 12:5 NASB)

As modern-day disciples of Christ, we are running in the same race—a race with challenges, trials, and different forces competing for our hearts, and specifically for the hearts of our children. The more we seek to understand the race, the better equipped we will be to train our children for success—not in the eyes of the world, but in the eyes of Christ.

Whether your child is eighteen months or eighteen years old, this book will guide you through the process of preparation for the "race" that awaits him in the secular world. It will also assure you that it is never too soon nor too late to begin this process.

PART 1

Defining the Race

If you have run with footmen and they have tired you out,
Then how can you compete with horses?
If you fall down in a land of peace,
How will you do in the thicket of the Jordan?
—Jeremiah 12:5 NASB

CHAPTER 1

Clarifying the Race

Before we delve into the specifics of how to prepare our children, it is important to acknowledge and understand the race itself, the multi-level, spiritual race that is the life we live. Several books of the Bible refer to life as a race. The analogy is a favorite of the apostle Paul who uses it in his letters to the Galatians, to the Corinthians, and to Timothy. But it is the prophet Jeremiah who presents the race in a way that, I believe, contains an important call to action for all parents: "If you have run with footmen and they have tired you out, then how can you compete with horses? If you fall down in a land of peace, how will you do in the thicket of the Jordan?" (Jeremiah 12:5 NASB).

When we place this verse in context, we find God speaking to Jeremiah, who has become fearful after receiving threats from a group of men of Anathoth (Jeremiah's hometown). God responds to Jeremiah's concerns with two challenging questions in which He implies, if you are weary from a small threat in a peaceful land, how will you fare in a foreign land filled with unknown dangers?

Did you notice that the verse mentioned two levels of the race: the "foot race" and then the "horse race"? We can equate the foot race with the portion of our lives that is lived in our comfort zones: settings in which it should be easy to be ourselves, to glorify Christ, and to speak of Him freely and without hesitation. In contrast, the horse race is the areas of our lives that are lived among unreceptive coworkers, liberal family members, and those who are opposed to Christ. For our children, the horse race is often the university or secondary schools. It's the tougher race, the real race of life. Do you remember the first time you realized you were "running with horses"? I do, and it isn't a great memory.

My first experience with the horse race came in my junior year of college during my physiology class. My professor, Dr. Washington, began a lecture making strong claims that our ancestors evolved from the oceanic waters, touting this origin of life theory called evolution as absolute truth. My heartbeat began to accelerate. I felt it was my duty to object, so I raised my hand. It was time to defend the truth. It was time to take a stand for the Lord.

Dr. Washington acknowledged my raised hand and asked, "Yes, Larry, do you have something to say?"

"Yes, sir," I responded. "I would like to respectfully disagree with your statements about evolution—I do not believe my ancestors came from fish." *Wow. That felt great,* I thought. I felt confident and thought for sure I was ready for the professor's response.

To my surprise, Dr. Washington said, "Please stand and take as long as you'd like to explain to the class what it is that you believe."

What? I thought to myself. *Did he just ask me to explain my point?* I had never been asked this before. My answer was over in twenty seconds. I didn't know what to say. I did not know how to defend my belief system. There I was, one of the leaders in my college youth group and considered strong in the faith by my peers, but I had nothing to say. I could disagree with the best of them. However, when someone put a microphone in my face, the foot-race training was exposed. I was shallow and gravely ill-prepared for the horse race. It wasn't love, sex, drugs, and rock 'n' roll that sent me spiraling that day; it was a horse by the name of Dr. Washington, a nice, intelligent, and articulate professor who knew what he believed.

This is the premise of this book. It is the rationale that changed the training plan for me and, a few years later, for my children. I realized that although I had been attending a great church, the depth of training did not match the intensity of the real world—the horse race. Was it possible that I, and we, had not even realized that there were two levels to the race of life? The flashing lights of caution were all around me. These lights illuminated a mound of research that unfortunately showed that I was one of many Christians who was falling short or, sadly, falling away altogether.

In his article, "The State of the Culture," in the *Faith & Family Values* magazine, Richard Land (2008) challenges the Christian community's awareness of the current biblical, moral, and cultural drift. Land clearly implies that the culture has had a greater influence on the Christian community than the Christian community has had on the culture. Using the salt and light metaphor found in the Gospel of Matthew 5:13-16, Land claims that it is the Christian community that has been salted and lit by the culture. Much of the contemporary research confirms the notion that there is a decline in religion in most Western countries. In fact, the religious preference group that has grown the most over the years in the United States is the one with no religious commitment (categorized as the *none* group) in the form of church attendance. The "none group" in the United States has grown from five percent in 1972 to fourteen percent in 2002. In nearly every country, including the United States, the secular group of *none* has increased over the past thirty years.

George Barna (1999) confirms that although most born again teenagers express confidence in their beliefs, many of their core beliefs are antithetical to biblical teaching, reflecting a societal trend toward unorthodox beliefs. Statistics from Barna convey that eighty-six percent of teens claim to be Christians, but only thirty-one percent claim to be absolutely committed and that only four percent of teenagers are classified as evangelicals (Barna, 2001). According to contemporary scholar Christian Smith (2005), thirty-eight percent of adolescents attend church weekly; sixteen percent attend one to two times per month; thirty-one percent attend rarely; and fifteen percent never attend. Examining twenty-year trends of twelfth-graders, there has been an eight percent decline in those who report weekly attendance; an increase of four percent who rarely attend; and a four percent increase in those who never attend religious services. It is interesting to note in Barna's 2001 study of adolescents that of the nineteen life goals and priorities, the highest rated items on the list were having a college degree, having good physical health, having close personal friendships, and having a comfortable lifestyle. Having a close relationship with God ranked eighth and being deeply committed to the Christian faith ranked fourteenth.

At this very moment, some of you are thinking that since you have young children this type of research does not apply to you. I could not encourage you enough not to fall prey to this notion. How we process the next few points related to one's worldview could actually set you on a proper course of preparation and training that will make all the difference when your child becomes a critically-thinking teenager. Later in the book I will be connecting this level of training for our children directly to the foundational years of early childhood. It is important to prepare our children for what they will be tempted to do. It is also essential to prepare them for what they will be encouraged to believe.

Weltanschauung

Josh McDowell says, "While we need to fear what our kids could be tempted to do, we need to be more concerned with what our kids are led to believe." McDowell's focus on one's belief system has become of great interest in the last twenty years. The term "worldview" is rooted in Immanuel Kant's German word *Weltanschauung*. Scottish theologian James Orr first introduced worldview thinking into Christian theology in the late nineteenth century. Orr's intent was to justify Christian belief by showing how Christianity connects to all of the important issues regarding worldview formation. Others contributed to the concept, but certainly the impact of Francis Schaeffer in the twentieth century on the establishment of the biblical Christian worldview is noteworthy. Schaeffer is credited as the one who elevated the importance of understanding Christianity as a total way of life. Schaeffer argued that all individuals have and operate from some particular worldview, and his discussions and writings on cultural issues from a Christian point of view serve as a catalyst for the worldview thought.

What is a worldview?

Sire (2004) defines worldview as a set of presuppositions that every individual holds about the world. He elaborates that a worldview is not just a set of basic concepts, but also a fundamental orientation of the heart, and more specifically, the biblical concept of the heart. The ancient Hebrew view of the heart was that it was the core of human personality, intellect, and religious life (Proverbs 2:6, 10; Exodus 4:14; 1 Chronicles 29:18). We also see that in the New Testament the heart is designated as the center of human affections, spiritual life, and intellect (John 14:1; Acts 8:21; Romans 1:21). The summary point for parents, and anyone else who has responsibilities in training children, is that our children's hearts must be considered when understanding the definition of worldview.

Contemporary Christian scholars contributing to the understanding and defining of the worldview concept include Nash, Colson, and Pearcey. Nash frames his definition of worldview around the content of a person's philosophical perspective. He argues that a person's understanding of the nature of God, reality, knowledge, morality, and man should be the foundation of one's worldview. Similarly, Colson and Pearcey provide an overall philosophic argument in that a worldview is an individual's sum total of beliefs about the world that directs daily decisions and actions. I like how Colson and Pearcey suggest that genuine Christianity, based on the truth of God's Word, is the only comprehensive way of examining and understanding reality, thus establishing it as a worldview. They emphasize that Christianity cannot be limited to a salvation experience, thus implying that one's worldview directs them through all of life's experiences. This is a critical point for parents. More specifically, remember my earlier example of Dr. Washington being the first "horse" I encountered? Yes, I had received Christ as my personal Lord and Savior—the salvation experience—but I had never really been trained to think critically about how life began, the origin of man, or how all of this reconciled with opposing beliefs.

There is a race, and it takes place in the marketplace of life far removed from the comfort areas of our homes and churches, and the race is intense. Competing for the minds and belief systems of our children is a man-centered philosophy founded on secularism. It is a battle of ideas. These ideas build one's worldview. In sections two and three, we will explore the specific ways in which you can incorporate intentional biblical training into your child's life so that his or her belief system is deliberately prepared.

God calls a time-out

What a setting! Moses is preparing to cross the Jordan River with the Israelites. God pulls Moses over to the bench for special instructions. It is paramount that we all understand and embrace God's instructions to Moses in Deuteronomy. It is important for parents, pastors, youth leaders, teachers, and basically everyone who invests in the training of the next generation. God's plan to train the next generation centered on parents. Based on Deuteronomy 6:6-7, the training of children is the primary responsibility of parents: "These words, which I am commanding you today, shall be on your heart. You shall teach them diligently to your sons and shall talk of them when you sit in your house and when you walk by the way and when you lie down and when you rise up" (Deuteronomy 6:6-7 NASB).

Take special notice that God did not place this responsibility on children's ministers or youth pastors or Christian schools or summer camps. He clearly directed Moses to tell Larry and Delinda that the belief system of Bryce, Luke, Zeke, and Chas (my four boys) is the number one priority. We certainly need the church and other training and educational models to assist us in the discipleship of our children, but there is no doubt that God places the whistles around the necks of parents as head coaches of their families.

Secondly, I want to pause and acknowledge a particular group of readers. I realize that some of you reading this book, like me, did not grow up in church or in a Christian home. My parents divorced when I was a baby, and I lived with my mother until my father was granted custody when I was seven.

9

From this point until graduation from high school, my family life consisted of non-Christian parents, extreme dysfunction, and an overall vacuum of anything remotely connected to God. I say this for the sole purpose of helping you understand that, regardless of your background, there is no doubt in my mind that through God's power you can become the head coach of your family and an essential part of training the next generation. And you must lead—the horses don't slow down for any reason.

Finally, Paul encourages us in Ephesians 5:15-16 to live purposefully. This word became more meaningful just weeks before our first child, Bryce, was born. Delinda and I were traveling from our home in Orlando to Cocoa Beach, Florida, where my grandparents lived. Grandma Taylor was very ill, and family members were coming in from everywhere to visit her. On the way, we came upon a horrific automobile accident—a semi-truck had hit a car head-on. The car was a complete pancake and debris was everywhere. I remember Delinda (nearly nine months pregnant) turning around in the car and looking back at the accident scene, saying, "I feel sorry for whoever was in that car."

After visiting Grandma in the hospital, we drove to her home where all the family was gathering. As we pulled into the driveway my Aunt Portia came outside—she was sobbing. She said, "Larry Alan, your dad has been killed in an accident." Instantly, I knew that the horrific accident we had driven by just a short time earlier was the actual scene of my father's death. I fell to my knees and wept. I learned that every day is important—we are not promised to see our spouse, children, friends, or family tomorrow. I committed that day to hug and kiss Delinda and my soon to be son every night as if it were the last time I would see them. We have 6,570 days with our children from birth to diploma—each day should be purpose-driven.

Chapter 1 Application

1. Reflect on your own spiritual journey. What specific training have you received in the area of worldview? (Books, conferences, etc.)

2. Based on Deuteronomy 6:6-8, what specific training do you provide for your children (including what you do or what you might hire others to do in order to help you)?

3. In what areas do you feel confident to train your children and in what areas do you feel inadequate?

CHAPTER 2

Thriving in the Thickets

Be on your guard; stand firm in the faith; be courageous; be strong.
—1 Corinthians 16:13 NIV

Turn with me again to Jeremiah 12:5. The end of the verse describes thickets surrounding the Jordan River. If you have not had the privilege of visiting the Holy Land, it is hard to imagine these thickets as more than low-lying underbrush along the river. The prophet Jeremiah would have immediately known that the thickets were deep, dark, and wild. Amidst the brambly trees and brush, lions and other predatory beasts lurked, awaiting the unsuspecting traveler.

Let's apply this analogy to the current culture of the United States. What do the thickets represent? I realize that the thickets facing our children are more intense as they grow older. Even if your child is only an infant, I would consider the time before he enters the thickets as a blessing: more time to prepare him for what lies ahead. What is amidst these thickets that awaits our children, unsuspecting or not? Indeed the obvious vices of the world will forever pose a sincere threat of entanglement to our youth culture—drugs, alcohol, and a culture that has saturated itself with a sensual and sexual nature. These vices are real, and we should never underestimate their destructive impact on the spiritual, physical, and emotional components of our children.

However, perhaps there are more potent influencers in the cultural thickets. The late Princeton theologian J. Gresham Machen pointed this out when he stated the following:

> *False ideas are the greatest obstacles to the reception of the gospel. We may preach with all the fervor of a reformer and yet succeed only in winning a straggler here and there, if we permit the whole collective thought of the nation to be controlled by ideas which prevent Christianity from being regarded as anything more than a harmless delusion. Under such circumstances, what God desires us to do is to destroy the obstacle at its root.* (William Lane Craig, 2004)

False ideas. How in the world could false ideas be on the same level of destruction as drugs or alcohol? Maybe this comment by the late philosopher Dr. Richard Rorty, University of Virginia, can provide insight. Rorty states:

> *Secular professors in the universities ought to arrange things so that students who enter as bigoted, homophobic religious fundamentalists will leave college with views more like our own. Students are fortunate to find themselves under the benevolent Herrschaft of people like me, and to have escaped the grip of their frightening, vicious, dangerous parents. We are going to go right on trying to discredit you [parents] in the eyes of our children, trying to strip your fundamentalist religious community of dignity, trying to make your views seem silly rather than discussable.*

There are "Dr. Rortys" in every university. One might think that my intention is to scare you to divert your children away from the Dr. Rortys of the world and to essentially avoid the thickets. Not only is that not my intention, it is in direct contrast to Jeremiah 12:5, as well as countless other biblical principles. I strongly believe that we need to prepare our sons and daughters to sit in the Dr. Rorty-led classrooms at the university—to thrive in the thickets. My oldest son, Bryce, graduated from Yale University (class of 2011); my second son, Luke, graduated from Princeton University (class of 2013), my third son, Zeke, attends the Film School of Florida State University (class of 2015); and Chas will be attending Rice University (Class of 2017). Needless to say, these universities are not known for being hospitable to the ideology derived from the Christian faith. My sons are running with the types of horses Jeremiah referenced.

Producing Acts 17 Disciples

Our goal as parents should be to produce *Acts 17 disciples; children who thrive in the thickets.* What is an Acts 17 disciple? In the seventeenth chapter of Acts, we see an excellent picture of what the outcome for our children should look like. Other than imitating Christ, as Paul encouraged us to do in Ephesians 5:1, we should aspire to imitate the apostle Paul as described in this brief scriptural narrative. In fact, these characteristics should be prevalent in all of our training paradigms found in the home, churches, and educational institutions. In this passage, we see Paul leaving the synagogue (not quite safe country for Paul, but for the purpose of our discussion let's assume that the synagogue, or church, represents a safe environment for our children) and immediately he is confronted by two opposing worldviews, the Epicureans and the Stoics (verse 18).

Has anything changed? Our children will someday leave our homes, and they will most likely be immediately confronted by opposing worldviews. Actually, over ninety percent of our children have already been trained in a similar secular educational model in the public school system. However, as Dr. Rorty clearly emphasized, the university is a more intense race. The horses are bigger, stronger, faster, and more experienced.

Notice that Paul did not retreat. He did not remain silent. He did not allow the intimidating environment of the city of Athens to send him back to the comfort of the foot race at church where everyone rallied around a similar belief system. I have often said that most Christians do two things when they are intimidated. They either retreat and thus create a vacuum of ideas based on truth, or they open their mouths and expose the vacuum of ideas based on truth. Both are bad. Paul did neither. Paul knew what he believed, and he had confidence to represent his faith in the pluralistic marketplace of the Athenian culture. He also knew what the Epicureans and Stoics believed. Paul reasoned and persuaded with some of the brightest minds and thinkers of his day—the Dr. Rortys. The result was twofold. Paul did not fall prey to empty deceit or philosophy (Colossians 2:6-8) but rather saw some who were in his midst profess Christ as their Lord (end of Acts 17). Paul was a clear illustration of one thriving in the thickets.

A disciple thinks differently

Developing an Acts 17 disciple results in children who think differently. There certainly is not a formula that guarantees results, but we do see characteristics in the Apostle Paul that are worthy of our aspirations. I often challenge parents to write on a three by five card the top characteristics they want their children to have when they are older, especially around the college age. In Acts 17, I see Paul imitating Christ and exhibiting a maturity that could serve as a very balanced three by five card goal sheet. What exactly constitutes an Acts 17 disciple? What does Paul do in Athens that applies to today? What can we glean from this narrative in Scripture that could help us train our children, whether in the developmental years of two to eight; the preteen years of nine to twelve; or the adolescent years of thirteen to eighteen?

- Paul was not afraid of the world.
- Paul understood the importance of taking every thought captive (2 Corinthians 10:5).
- Paul developed discernment by "practicing" (Hebrews 5:14).
- Paul developed the attitude of Christ (Philippians 2:2-11), knowing that he was to love and serve Christ.

Too many eighteen- to twenty-four-year-olds are drifting in their faith

Late adolescence has been historically placed in the age range of eighteen to twenty-two and characterized by adolescents' tendency to explore their worldview and religious beliefs and critically analyze their parents' beliefs. In many ways, college students become seekers in that they are exposed to new information by faculty members and others who are expressing different values and religious perspectives. These characteristics have been supported by UCLA's Higher Education Research Institute (HERI), which conducted one of the most comprehensive longitudinal research projects for this age group. The HERI study claims that twenty-three percent of entering freshmen in the fall of 2004 labeled themselves seekers, and that over fifty percent of them have different views on spiritual and religious matters than their family members (Astin, 2004).

One of the largest current studies of adolescent spiritual beliefs is The National Study of Youth and Religion. Indicating continued biblical worldview drift, the opposite of thriving in the thickets, this study was analyzed by Christian Smith, who claims that youth are not on a spiritual journey but simply on a continual path in the faith traditions of their families. He summarizes his concern about this drift by stating that adolescents embrace *moralistic therapeutic deism*, implying that these moral principles have not been internalized into core values.

Thus, it is interesting to observe that precisely when our children are entering the university, they are also entering a phase of exploration of their own belief system and worldview. The reason our children are exploring their belief system at this age could be related to how they have been trained (lack of biblical worldview training before age eighteen coupled with a secular-based training provided by the public school systems where most Christian young people attend). Many opinions and a growing amount of research relate to this issue. For the purpose of this book, however, and to our point of preparing Acts 17 children who thrive in the thickets, we will remain focused on the training plan that precedes the entrance into the university. The one thing on which we all agree is the importance of transmitting a biblical worldview to the next generation. The university might seem too far away to begin worrying about your child walking away from our faith. However, I am proposing to you that parents should consider being more intentional in their training long before their children reach this age.

Focusing on the next generation

It is relatively safe to assume that parents and church leaders who adhere to the Christian faith are inherently interested in promoting and preserving their community's ethic. One of the primary parenting goals is to encourage children to preserve the family's faith. In *Kingdom Ethics*, Glen Stassen and David Gushee (2003) define a worldview as a cohesive set of beliefs through which people view the world and thus, consciously or not, set their life-course. Stassen and Gushee state,

> *A community's ethic flows from, and includes, the core worldview convictions through which that community interprets reality and defines the good life. We are claiming that Christian ethics must be self-consciously grounded in well-conceived theological convictions, fundamentally the vision of the reign of God. This is our worldview, our driving meta-narrative; if it is not, we are quite likely grounding our living on some other fundamental worldview and thus straying from our loyalty to Jesus Christ. Worldview helps shape character, and character overflows into action (p. 63).*

Stassen and Gushee argue that it takes community to shape a person with integrity of character, and that Christian thinkers in recent years have come to recognize that the cultural moral drift with which we are so concerned is a worldview issue. They argue that developing a Christian worldview, and subsequently shaping one's integrity and character, requires a community effort that not only elevates the theological framework, but also counters the man-centered worldview espoused in a mainstream pluralistic society. I would propose that the key to this transmission of our belief system, and thus the thriving component, is adjusting the training process, adjusting the way our Christian community shapes the integrity, character, and belief system of our children.

Chapter 2 Application

1. Using a three by five index card, write down four or five characteristics you desire for your child when he or she is twenty-two to twenty-five years old.

2. What are some current and future experiences that your children will encounter that will expose them to false ideas?

3. Following up on the community concept of Stassen and Gushee, does any part of your child's community have a different worldview than yours? If so, what can you do to counter these opposing ideas?

CHAPTER 3

Reversing the Trend: Four Essential Elements

*See to it that no one takes you captive through hollow and
deceptive philosophy, which depends on human tradition
and the basic principles of this world rather than Christ.*
—Colossians 2:8 (NIV)

Early in my teaching and coaching career, I was privileged to
become a head coach of our boys' basketball team. You would
have been impressed with my practice sessions. They were very
organized, structured, and purposeful. Our practices were
designed to cover the full spectrum of what a team needed
to know, including a commitment to the fundamentals. It all
sounds good, but did you notice what I left out? What I did not
mention was how my team did in the games. We got killed!
When we actually competed against other schools, we were
embarrassed. The season was long, but there was one bright
spot. I learned something that season that changed my entire
perspective on parenting, education, and sports.

The intensity of my practices did not match the intensity of the game

I needed to change my practice strategy and routine. Yes, those organized, structured, and purpose-driven practices would have impressed you. However, my practices simply did not come close to resembling the real game. My players were not being prepared adequately. And since the object of the game was to compete and to win, I had no choice but to make adjustments to how my players were being trained. I needed not only to help them understand our team book, philosophy, and game plan; I also needed to help them understand what they were going to be competing against. Additionally, I needed them to experience intense sessions in practice so the game was relatively routine. Rarely after that season did an opposing coach or team beat us due to strategy or intensity. We still lost games, but our new training method put us in a much better competitive situation—we were ready and rarely surprised.

Our practice sessions with our children need to change

In many ways we are still training our children today the same way we trained them a generation ago. I stated in chapter one that the premise of this book is to suggest an adjustment to our training process. I attempted to present a case for this claim based on two things—the high attrition rate of eighteen to twenty-two-year-olds from the faith or the church, and this same age group's shallow grasp of biblical literacy and worldview. Our practice sessions should be preparing our children to enter this world with confidence, courage, and conviction. If seventy to ninety percent of kids are walking away from their faith, something is wrong, or incomplete, with our practices.

As Jesus commissioned His disciples to take the Gospel into the world, He knew they would face intense opposition. If we want to expand and sustain the Christian ethic and worldview—if we want to equip our children to "run with the horses," then we collectively must elevate and maintain a more compelling level of training and discipleship. Parents and churches have 6,570 days with our children before they typically enter the university (not that parenting ends at eighteen)! The research is clearly pointing out that the depth of our training during this time does not match the intensity of the culture they are entering.

Adjusting the training method must begin at home

Nearly every time the subject of training and discipleship comes up, the rocks start getting thrown at the church. Although I think today's church training strategies need to focus more on discipleship, I disagree that the problem is the church. How can we expect the two hours spent in church on Sundays to counteract the effect that countless hours of culture saturation have had upon our children? The average eighteen-year-old who has been active in church will have spent approximately 2,500 hours in church, while spending over 16,000 hours in school. This does not even include the thousands of hours our children spend away from church or family such as with their friends and peer group or using social media and other forms of media entertainment. So first, we must stop relying completely on the church to train our children.

Remember Deuteronomy 6:7-8? God instructed Moses that parents were to be the primary trainers. You know your children better than any pastor ever will. You have the whole context of your child's heart and life. A pastor will almost always have a limited knowledge of exactly how your child's life is going or the condition of that child's heart. Using the four posterity pillars from Luke 2:52 (wisdom, stature, and favor with God and man), your holistic view of your children will always be more complete. You have more observational data to process how your child is doing in these four areas. Certainly, parents should rely on assistance from pastors or teachers, but at the end of the day it is Mom and Dad who should be developing and monitoring the training plan for their children.

I believe there are four essential elements to consider as we address strategically how to reverse the trend:

1. Understanding the discipleship process after children become Christians (before college)
2. Understanding that discipleship continues to take place during college and after college (the three phase "race" cycle)
3. Linking the parents' faith to the next generation (the Psalm 78 principle)
4. Creating an impact by uniting the home, church, and school (creating synergy through a congruent message).

In many ways the Christian community has lost its focus on these four concepts as evidenced by the mainstream training models found in our churches and homes as well as the twenty to thirty year drifting trend. I would argue that the first step in reversing this trend is the recognition of these four concepts.

Understanding the discipleship process after my children have become Christians and before they enter the university

It is fundamental that we understand the difference between the road to Damascus and the road to the agora. What is Damascus and what is the agora? Damascus represents conversion. Paul was converted while on the road to Damascus. In today's context, this would represent our child's personal decision to follow Christ. This decision to follow Christ is something that we as parents earnestly and consistently pray for from the very moment of our child's birth. Beyond prayers, the road to Damascus is marked by ceremonies, rituals, and celebratory events depending on one's denomination and culture. Conversion is the first step to the end goal. It is undoubtedly one of the most significant experiences for parents.

I have been honored to pray with each of my four sons during their personal conversion to Christ. In fact, three of my boys surrendered their lives to Christ while sitting in my lap in the same chair that I sat in when I surrendered my life to Christ as a high school student. In the auditorium at Blue Ridge Assembly at a Fellowship of Christian Athletes national conference, I accepted Christ as my personal Lord and Savior. My road to Damascus was different than their roads, but our conversions had similar outcomes. As a Christian school administrator for the past twenty-five years, it has been such a blessing for me to share hundreds of these conversion stories with other parents and their children.

The road to the agora is different

Agora means "the marketplace," specifically, the meeting place for the ancient Greeks. It was at this meeting place, the agora, where business was conducted, issues were discussed and debated, and the ideologies of the culture were formed and dispersed. Within the context of this book and the topic of reversing the worldview drifting trend, the agora represents the university and beyond to the epicenters of cultural forming entities—Hollywood, Wall Street, Washington, DC, and the like.

The road to Damascus is part one of the Great Commission (Matthew 28:19-20) and certainly the prerequisite to making disciples. However, part two of Jesus' charge to make disciples is the teaching and training element—preparing for the road to the agora. I believe the Christian community has done and continues to do an exceptional job at the evangelical part of the Great Commission. It is the dominant thread of all efforts in every denomination. I don't think these efforts should ever decrease—if anything, they should increase. However, I would also argue that the drifting trend overwhelmingly is connected to the lack of strategic effort on teaching and training—discipleship. Preparing our children for the agora is the most neglected aspect of discipleship for parents and the church. Research supports this claim. Too many of our converts and children are walking away from the church. The agora is eating them up and spitting them out.

Recognizing this is essential to any potential change in our parent and church training paradigm. Presently, I believe we are on the front end of a movement that has recognized a need to change how we train our children. There is a massive movement going on in this country, and parents are leading it. Parents are embracing Deuteronomy 6:7-8 and are beginning to take responsibility for the training of their children. They are heeding the warning signs of the secular drift in our youth culture. They are changing the culture of their homes, their churches, and even their educational strategies. For several years, the fastest growing segments of education have been homeschooling and Christian schools. Most denominational leaders and pastors have not been on the front end of this movement. The road to the agora will require churches to change.

Understanding that the discipleship of my children continues during their college years and even beyond college—the three-phase cycle of transmitting our faith to the next generation

The first phase is marked by the 6,570 days from birth to high school diploma. The second phase is the 1,500 days during the four years of college. The third phase is life: work, marriage, and parenting. Of course, this is a simplified model of a much more complex array of spiritual, emotional, and physical maturity points. Grasping these three phases and the specific training needs during each one will help us get our arms around an ongoing discipleship plan. Later in the book, I will address specific points of this cycle in relationship to the role of parents and the church in training the next generation. The primary point is that the maturity cycle for Christians does not end when one graduates from high school or college. The maturity cycle is naturally different for every person; however, there are training points along the way that certainly increase the probability of transmitting one's faith to one's children.

Linking our faith to the "children yet to be born," our grandchildren (Psalm 78 principle)

It is this principle that serves as the transcendent purpose for all parenting practices. It is foundational. It establishes the marching orders for parents and the curriculum for this process. Take some time to read Psalm 78. Notice God's plan for parents—to tell the great stories of God to their children. Notice the curriculum—the great stories of God. What are the great stories of God? The creation, the fall, and redemption are all truths found in His Word. The great stories of God communicate the entire story, meta-narrative, a complete biblical worldview.

The gold nugget in this passage is found in verse six: ". . . even the children yet to be born"—our grandchildren. This clearly recognizes that our training is the key to passing the baton of faith to the next generation. In other words, we are not training children . . . we are training "child—raisers."

Notice that it is the parents' responsibility. Of course, pastors, children's ministries, Christian schools, and para-church organizations are important and have scriptural admonitions to assist parents in the discipleship of children. But the biblical model for transmitting our faith to the next generation requires parents to take the lead. I believe that churches need to help equip parents to do the job that God has commanded them to do through discipleship training and by providing helpful resources, including curriculum, books, and classes.

Creating the amazing impact that occurs when the home, church, and school are working together on the discipleship process of our children (creating synergy by establishing congruence, or a common message)

Synergy comes from the Greek word *synergia,* meaning cooperation and joint work. The important result of synergy is that the outcome is of more value than the sum of the parts. I think we would all agree that the outcome from our current training paradigm needs a greater value. More specifically, we need to reverse the attrition rate of our eighteen to twenty-two-year-olds from their faith; we need to increase the depth of biblical worldview for all young adults; and overall, we need to change the trend of secularism and its impact on the Christian community. In other words, when you add up the various training components in the life of a typical Christian young person (what parents do with their children; what churches do within their children's and youth ministries; and what weekday education does), their cooperative efforts should add a greater value, due to synergy, than the sum of their individual efforts.

I believe the research clearly suggests we are not reaching the level of synergy needed to reverse the trend. In fact, the first step to reaching synergy is a cooperative effort. When was the last time churches and parents and schools adopted a cohesive training plan characterized by well-defined roles, goals, and objectives? For nearly ninety-six percent of the Christian community whose children are educated in public schools, it is pretty much impossible to develop a joint effort with the school to develop the child's worldview. Even when you only examine the home and the church, you rarely see a united effort. The church has a plan, and the parents have a plan. Actually, according to Barna, "Parents are not so much unwilling to provide more substantive training to their children as they are ill-equipped to do such work" (Barna, 2003). Few churches have a coherent training plan within their educational system. The children's ministers do their thing, and the youth pastors do their thing. I am not suggesting that what they do is bad, I am only pointing out that they rarely work together, thus synergy is not reached.

Here is my point—how can we even reach the point of synergy if our training entities (home, church, and school) do not work together and even within their own entities, they are often fragmented? This is a huge issue and one that is not easily fixed. If we wish to reverse the trend, I don't think we have an option. When this point is broached I usually begin hearing the "boos" from the different groups. The pastors are offended, parents feel scolded, and heaven forbid anyone touches the sacred cow—our school system. To get us out of the emotional state of this discussion and into a more objective state, I would like to unpack my assertions.

What does the research say about the key influences in worldview formation?

The bottom line is that the transmission of one's values, beliefs, and worldview comes from a variety of sources. The *social learning theory* suggests that children develop attitudes and behaviors by observing the actions of parents and significant others who serve as role models. One's family, neighborhood, church group, peers, and school are examples of the multiple influences on our child's belief system. Regnerus (2004) calls this the "linked-lives" paradigm. In other words, we know that there is research that credits parents, peers, church education, teachers, quality level and type of education, and intentional worldview training as collectively having an impact on the worldview and belief system of young adults.

Don't miss this point; it may be the single most important point in this book. Did you notice how many points of impact on worldview development are credited in the literature? The research is telling us that all of the training entities are essential. And it is telling us that there should be no islands. Please allow me to be very direct. What this is saying to pastors and youth leaders and parents and Sunday school teachers and Christian school leaders is that we need each other—we need synergy. Synergy develops when we work together. And when we consider what is at stake—the development and transmission of a biblical worldview from this generation to the next—we see the stakes are high. But let me continue to support my claims.

We know that parents are the primary molders of their children's values and belief system, and that the peer group also plays an important role.

There is some truth in the adage that it takes a village to socialize a child's Christian-based worldview. However, Boyatzis and Janicki (2003) claim that the family is the first village. The study on adolescent beliefs and values development by Regnerus, et al. (2004), the "linked-lives" theory, emphasizes that young people are developing and functioning in a dynamic and reciprocal way with their environments, including relationships with other people, groups, and subcultures. Though parents continue to be the primary influence in shaping their children's values and overall spiritual formation, Regnerus claims that peers and schoolmates also play a significant role. Erickson's (1992) significant implication for parents is to model beliefs and values at home, as well as clearly and firmly direct the children into activities that ensure socialization into a similar worldview. He concludes that the parental influence of directing their children, known as channeling, to other social influences during adolescent years actually places them in environments where their core beliefs are either enhanced or not. This implication correlates with Gunnoe and Moore's (2002) longitudinal study in which peers emerge as a better predictor than parents on beliefs and values predictors for seventeen to twenty-two-year-olds.

Church education impacts one's worldview.

In addition to parents and peers being credited as molders of worldview for children, the church, and primarily the youth ministry of the church, serves as another influencer.

Shirley (2002) concludes that there are three significant predictors of students having higher Christian orthodoxy (doctrine) scores: the degree of Sunday school participation, family interaction, and consistency of personal devotions. The researcher also notes that the three working together (Sunday school, family interaction, and personal devotion) achieve the optimal results. Another interesting finding is that the degree of participation in spiritual training activities at home appears to be the factor dividing those who have higher or lower orthodoxy scores. The synergy between church and home appears to be a significant factor in establishing strong orthodoxy (understanding the essential doctrines of the Christian faith).

Teachers have an impact on the worldview formation of children.

More specifically, the personal worldview and belief system of teachers plays a pivotal role. Richard Riesen (2002) notes that the intellectual development of students is not separated from their spiritual and worldview development. Riesen also points out that essentially no education takes place in a worldview-free vacuum. Fyock's (2007) research, *The Effect Of The Teacher's Worldviews on the Worldviews of High School Seniors,* is guided by the inquiry of whether or not a teacher's worldview affects the worldview of high school students. Statistical testing suggests that seniors' worldviews move toward the faculty's worldviews. This study indicates that a course taught from a biblical Christian worldview by an experienced faculty member increases biblical understanding on several worldview issues.

If teachers impact one's worldview, naturally, the type of education impacts worldview.

Researchers have long recognized that schools are powerful environments that shape one's worldview. Deckard and Smithwick's (2002) research suggested a strong correlation between having a biblical Christian worldview and the type of school a student attends. The implication is that students tend to adopt the worldview of the teachers who teach them. I am not claiming that sending your children to a Christian school will guarantee that they will develop a biblically-based worldview—in fact, there is research that suggests that not all Christian schools have the same positive impact on a child's spiritual development.

Regardless of Christian school, home school, or public school, the bottom line is that the research is showing us that the majority of our Christian students are receiving an inadequate education (defined as a lack of biblical worldview training). Students who are not receiving adequate biblical worldview training are entering college with a weak foundation. Sutton (1997) advances a claim that an erosion of belief in the existence of objective religious truth characterizes this age group. His findings include that over one half of the students studied reflect ambivalence and confusion regarding the need for explicit faith in Christ to receive salvation.

I am not trying to tell you where to send your kids to school.

However, I have no problem discussing the sacred cow to most Christians—the child's school system. I am simply providing empirical research. Indeed, this is a lightning rod issue. There are those who vehemently argue against pulling children out of the public schools. They base this argument primarily on the salt and light principle. Although I strongly feel that this salt and light claim is not only a weak position, I also think it is a biblical reference used out of context. Indeed, the process of discipleship includes placing our disciples amongst the world, but I have seen very few children, if any, who are true disciples (spiritually mature followers of Christ). I choose not to enter the debate of where we should send our children to school. However, I will gladly dialogue over the biblical principles of training our children as well as the compelling research pointing to the secularization of Christians.

I don't think secular schools are the cause of worldview drift in the Christian community—that is too simple a charge to a complex process of transmitting our worldview. Too many parents and churches have proven that they can transmit a worldview to their children in spite of the secular worldview training of the public schools. However, there is no arguing that a dualistic training paradigm has potentially devastating results on one's worldview. Dividing life into different parts (secular Monday through Friday at school and Christian on Sunday at church) and navigating through life by operating each part from a different worldview has proven to fragment one's belief system.

We must respectfully create dialogue over these four essential elements as we strategically address how to reverse the trend. Everyone must be invited to the dialogue table. It is not enough to develop isolated plans. The lack of religious congruence (primarily within the context of the personal relationship between child and parent) has a negative impact on the overall condition of one's faith. It is this specific congruence, between parent and child, on which we will focus in Chapter Four—creating synergy between parent and child through specific family practices.

Chapter 3 Application

1. Read Psalm 78:6. In relationship to training and discipleship, what do you consider when you think about your grandchildren?

2. Barna's research stated that eighty-nine percent of parents do not feel adequate in training children. In what areas do you feel adequate or inadequate when it comes to child-training? How could you improve in these areas?

3. Reflecting on the three primary training entities, home, church, and school, do you feel there is a congruent message or worldview for your child? If not, which of the three does not support your worldview or values?

4. What is your plan to present a congruent message to your child?

PART 2

Creating Deliberate Practices for the Race

And Jesus grew in wisdom and stature,
and in favor with God and man.
—Luke 2:52 NIV

CHAPTER 4

Synergy-Creating Practices

The student is not above the teacher, but everyone who is fully trained will be like their teacher.
—Luke 6:40 NIV

Reversing the trend will require a proactive training strategy for our children. We can understand the Psalm 78 principle and the need to prepare our children for the road to the agora and be fully committed and aware of the three-phase race cycle; but if we do not heed the biblical mandate on training our children and the bountiful research that describes the role of parents, peers, teachers, church education, and weekday education and ultimately make some significant adjustments to the overall training paradigm, there will be no reversal. The concept of synergy was discussed in the last chapter, and it was based on the importance of all of the influencing agents of a child's worldview and belief system developing a congruent message—what parents are emphasizing at home is also the same as the core values being nurtured at church, in the child's peer group, and throughout their weekday educational programs. It begins in the home.

If I told you that certain practices served as predictors for children to continue in their faith throughout the turbulent adolescent and young adult stages, would that interest you?

Sure it would. And if I told you that you did not have to have a degree in theology to lead your family through these practices, would that encourage you? Sure it would. The practices I am talking about are based on abundant research, and they are doable in everyday life routines—if they are a priority and if you are intentional about them.

I strongly believe that the biblical principle of Luke 6:40 is the most powerful principle related to the practices I am suggesting.

In other words, the influence of parents is immeasurable in the areas of Bible reading, Bible study, and prayer. These practices can be administered to some degree by other people, such as youth pastors, teachers, other parents, and peers; however, we are talking about reaching synergy levels—and there simply is no replacement for Mom and Dad. Luke 6:40 would encourage me to develop these practices with my children so that the most important influencers in their lives truly mold them: parents.

Children will look like you—Mom and Dad!

Multiple studies suggest that children's observational learning may lead them to share their parents' values, attitudes, and behaviors. The bottom line is that youth tend to resemble their parents in spiritual values. Lee, Rice, and Gillespie (1997) pose a research question of how patterns of family worship relate to the behaviors and beliefs of adolescents, again focusing on the fact that parents play the vital role in the development of their children's belief system. The obvious inference here is that we must carefully consider: What does our spiritual condition look like? Do we look like Christ?

Do you want your children to adopt your values and moral absolutes?

Early research from Willits and Crider (1989) claims that exposure to the parents' advanced moral reasoning is not enough to influence adolescents, but the relationship with them is the necessary ingredient. In other words, we can preach all we want about the many moral absolutes based on God's Truth, such as purity in relationships, the sanctity of life, etc., but what increases the probability of your children internalizing and adhering to these absolutes is their relationship with you. Our sermons are not as impactful unless we have bonded with our kids.

What are the synergy-creating practices?

There are, of course, many practices embedded into the four below, but these serve as foundational ones. Notice that they all revolve around you, the parent. They do not include outside influences such as children's and youth ministries or Christian schools or para-church ministries. This is all about the dynamic of family, home, and the relationship we develop with our children. In order to maximize the full effect of the Luke 6:40 principle, we must elevate the parent/child relationship. What does the research say about this relationship and these practices?

1. *Communication and emotional closeness*—how we converse with our children through discussions and conversations that are interactive and not dominated by Mom and Dad; understanding that the child's personality has a lot to do with communication strategies; how our children perceive the depth of the emotional bond and unconditional love and support even through strictness and disciplinary moments

2. *Family rituals*—daily, weekly, and annual routines; relationship-building practices that are prioritized in the midst of the busyness of life; sacred spiritual times that are integrated into normal family life
3. *Parenting style*—how we oversee and manage our children; the style and personality of the parent during daily interaction with children; how we motivate, encourage, monitor, discipline and direct our children
4. *Dealing with conflict*—the process to which we adhere when conflict hits the home; connecting conflict to the other practices such as communication in order to honor the principle of unity and peace and yet deal with opportunities of personal growth.

Developing emotional closeness through communication

The emotional closeness between the parent and child and its influence on the transmission of core values is the primary key to passing on your faith. Regnerus and Burdette's (2006) research on religious change and family dynamics shows that children who feel emotionally close to their parents are positively impacted in adolescent spiritual practices. They claim that the lack of religious congruency may correspond with a variety of poor relationship outcomes and vice versa. The warmth and support between the parent and child are crucial in the transmission process. Sensitive and responsive parenting enhances opportunities for observational (your children observing you) learning and the transmission of norms and expectations.

Communication is certainly not the only factor in building a close relationship but it is one of the most important links to closeness. The primary thing to remember is that the communication needs to go both ways. One-way talking is pretty typical in most parent-child dialogues but it is not the best way to ensure that your children will value your input, beliefs, and opinions. Creating dialogue by asking open-ended questions is a practice easily integrated into everyday life. Evening prayer time and family devotions, coming home from school or church, and during mealtime are all opportunities to create two-way dialogue.

The parent-child communication process dealing with core values has a reciprocal quality. Essentially, the relationship between parent and child is enhanced by conversations marked by children's active participation and expression of their ideas and the parents' openness to those ideas. Sustained discourse between parents and children on beliefs and values strongly relates to the actual transmission of beliefs and values to the children. Talking *with* our children and not *to* them is the key point. Many parents are nervous about asking open-ended questions, especially as the children get older—but it is essential.

Family practices that build the relationship

It seems so simple, but sharing spiritual practices and informal fun activities with the family is one of the most important rituals we can do. Praying and doing family devotions together and routinely having biblical discussions are considered some of the most profound influencing activities in which parents can invest. Shared religious activities contribute to intimacy and commitment in overall family cohesion, which is considered the central link of close relationships. The bottom line is that the children's acquisition of values is based on the parent-child relationship; this is paramount in the actual transmission process.

Developing daily, weekly, and annual rituals that elevate God's Word, emphasize the family unit regularly, and create venues that accommodate spiritual growth, serve as an incubator for synergy. The synergy from personal relationships between parents and children will ultimately impact the child's internalization of the desired belief system.

It is important to note that not all times need to be spiritual in nature

I say this carefully because I do not want to suggest a dualistic training plan where the spiritual is relegated to church services and Bible studies. I think if you surveyed the four Taylor boys and asked them what their greatest memories are related to rituals and family practices, they would mention Dunkin' Donuts and our annual family conference in the mountains. Early in my parenting, I was looking for a weekly activity and when I found it, I stuck with it for nearly twelve years. The result—hundreds of visits to Dunkin' Donuts! What did we do? Get ready, this is deep. Every Saturday morning I took the boys to get a doughnut—I discovered an age-old secret: you are an instant hero when sprinkled donuts are involved. I still have pictures of the Dunkin' Donut ladies picking my boys up and taking them back to the sink to spray the icing off of their faces and bodies. We had a blast—and Mom loved having Saturday mornings off!

I will never forget Dr. Ward (one of my colleagues) telling me that parents at our school were wondering where I was on Saturday mornings and why I was not attending the soccer games. I was the athletic director at the school, and it was pretty noticeable that I was absent from the games. I encouraged Dr. Ward to tell the parents that they could find me on the corner of Orange Avenue and Kaley Street at the Dunkin'

Donuts, spending time with my boys. Family rituals need to be guarded from anything that is of lesser importance—including work. Our ritual was simple and inexpensive, but magical in building a loving relationship with my boys—not to mention that I loved the coffee and apple fritters!

Not too long ago I received a phone call from Bryce. Like many college students, he had slept in on Saturday morning and missed his meal-plan breakfast. He decided to walk to a nearby Dunkin' Donuts. At first, I didn't get why Bryce was calling. In fact, it took Delinda (my wife) to explain—he was remembering our good old days when we visited the doughnut shop together. Since that day, I have received multiple phone calls from Bryce on his way to Dunkin' Donuts—amazing that a sprinkled doughnut can have such an impact.

A twenty-seven year tradition in the mountains—and the "chair"

Delinda and I started attending a family conference the first year of our marriage. The Fellowship of Christian Athletes sponsored the conference—I was a coach, and I wanted to meet other coaches and let Delinda meet their wives. Little did I know we would attend this same conference for twenty-seven straight years. Our boys loved going to the beautiful mountains of North Carolina every year. Not only did this conference provide Delinda and me an annual tune-up for our marriage, it became a ritual for our boys. This was the same mountain and conference center that I discussed earlier, where I, as a high school athlete, had accepted Christ and the same mountain with the same chair where three of my four boys prayed to accept Christ. Every year we visit that chair and read Psalm 78. It is our ceremony of gratefulness to God . . . a significant spiritual marker for our family.

I will never forget the first time one of our boys had to miss the family camp due to a college obligation. We called him when we stopped at the hotel en route to the mountain and told him how much we missed him. I grabbed the phone, and although I meant well, I said something insensitive. I jokingly told him that at dinnertime at Cracker Barrel (one of our traditional stops), we had more hot biscuits and honey since he wasn't there to eat them. A few minutes later Delinda motioned to me that he was quite upset, and I think even a few tears were shed—the biscuits triggered a flood of great memories he was missing. I had no idea how important this trip was for my boys and our family—and it wasn't Disney World, it was a simple family conference that had created a deep bond within our hearts.

Parenting style

It may not seem like a practice, and technically it is not, but parenting style has such a unique connection to the overall transmission of values and beliefs that I have included it in this section. There are three major parenting styles—authoritarian, authoritative, and permissive. The unique aspect of each parenting style is how it can affect the other practices that help to produce synergy. Depending on one's style, the child of this parent could be more interested in what the parents believe and feel closer emotionally to this parent.

1. *Authoritarian*—"my way or the highway"; strict, with little to no support; drill sergeant
2. *Authoritative*—a balance of strict and supportive
3. *Permissive*—support only; little to no strictness

Peterson's (2006) research project on generativity (linking one's faith to the next generation) and successful parenting focused on the parent-child relationship and linked the authoritative parenting style to an increased chance of transmitting religious beliefs and practices to their children. Several other studies also suggest that the authoritative parenting correlates to high adolescent spiritual commitment. Parents who balance support with strictness have a greater chance that their child will continue in the faith.

On the contrary, dogmatic parenting styles (authoritarian) strongly related to alienation from their parents' spiritual beliefs. This rigid style has proven to be the most ineffective of the three. On the opposite end of the spectrum is the other ineffective parenting style: permissive. Emotional support without boundaries and discipline characterizes this style. This method serves as a potential link to the negative peer influence because when parents are weak in monitoring their children, those kids have a greater likelihood of joining high-risk peer groups. This research has to be taken into consideration when examining Regnerus and Burdette's (2006) study on religious change and adolescent family dynamics, which indicates that the frequency of church service attendance tends to decline between eighth and twelfth grades. In other words, parenting style can impact the type of peer group a child gravitates toward at a time when church attendance is on the decline, which is not a good combination.

Personally, I brought a lot of baggage into my marriage and in particular in the category of parenting style. What about you? I was raised in a divorced situation and grew up with my dad—the ultimate authoritarian. It was always "his way or the highway" with little to no emotional support. So, guess what I struggled with early in my parenting? I was too strict with my boys without providing the support they needed. Early in my parenting, I was fortunate to be counseled and encouraged to submit all of my past to the Lord. I praise God for how He molded a new parenting style in me. I want to encourage you to inspect yourself in this area and seek the One who can conduct a supernatural adjustment. Slight tweaks in this area could make a significant difference in the transmission of your faith to your children.

Dealing with conflict

Every family has issues. Regardless of spiritual depth, number of children, gender, or age, there is conflict. Wherever there are people, there will be moments and even seasons of disunity. The biblical principle of unity applies to our families, not just the church. Reaching a point of synergy requires a steady commitment to handling conflict. Although there are multiple scenarios that create conflict, I want to focus primarily on the situations when a child disagrees with his parent. I want to provide a biblical model that can be used to train your children to respectfully disagree with you and how to state their opinions, requests, or appeals. This model should be adapted according to a child's age but the principles are timeless and universal with all authority figures, including teachers, coaches, and future bosses.

First, some important givens: some children are compliant in nature and some are strong-willed. Rarely do you have to wonder what your strong-willed child is thinking—he or she has no problem letting you know. This is not the case with your compliant child. Rarely do you know what is on that child's mind because of his or her agreeable temperament. The simple truth, though, is that the compliant child is still disagreeing with you. Regardless of how God wired our children, they all need guidance in how to properly share their opinions. Second, without proper coaching in this area, we may actually be thwarting some discussion. Authoritarian parents really struggle with implementing this model. How we deal with conflict directly correlates with the synergy practice of communication and relationship-building that is important in the transmission of our belief system. And, finally, just because your child disagrees with you, it does not mean he is a heathen—this is natural. The manner in which he disagrees with you and other authority figures is the key.

I call this the "biblical appeal process." Do you remember Jesus in the garden? Just hours before His torturous death, Jesus made an appeal to His Father. I believe there are several points to His appeal that we can use as we train our children. Let me provide the outline first and then describe it. The model is simple in presentation but obviously difficult to implement.

1. *Notice where Jesus was: the setting*—He was alone.
2. *Notice the tone in His voice*—He was respectful, not argumentative.
3. *Notice His posture and body language*—He was humble and respectful, on His knees.
4. *Notice His presentation or appeal*—He made His request but accepted His Father's will.

I am not suggesting that you train your kids to get on their knees when they want to disagree with you—not at all. What I am highly recommending is to train your children to do something they will need to apply throughout their lifetime—learn how to deal respectfully with authority figures. The end goal is to build strong relationships with our children. Conflict is inevitable. The "biblical appeal process" is simply a guide, or a process, that we should begin implementing when our children are young. We need to train them to respectfully request some discussion time over something or a decision that is bothering them. They need to know that their body language and tone of voice and overall spirit (regardless of the final decision) is essential for an appeal. They also need to know that you care about what is on their minds and that you are willing to talk things through. Arguing should not be permitted. Appeals and talking through differences of opinions should be encouraged. They are excellent opportunities to coach your children on issues. They are also invitations to hear what is really going on in their minds and hearts.

I conclude this chapter with one final thought and challenge

Creating synergy in the home is the key part of the entire Great Commission (Matthew 28:19-20) formula. The end goal of our time here on earth is to create disciples. Disciples make strong churches. Strong churches make better communities and overall culture. Some would argue that the evangelical community has focused more on building strong churches than on building strong homes. A strong church should be measured by a strong discipleship program and not solely by church attendance. The Great Commission is not just about evangelizing the lost; it also includes a vibrant discipleship program. I would argue that our greatest need is to train parents to disciple their children—without synergy in the home, the church will never reach its maximum potential of honoring one of the most important mandates in Scripture: the Great Commission. Moms and dads focusing on their parenting style, proper communication skills, family rituals and routines, and dealing with conflict are foundational to creating the synergy needed for the making of a disciple of Christ.

Chapter 4 Application

1. How do you look spiritually? Based on the Luke 6:40 principle (your children will look like you spiritually), what areas of your personal spiritual life need the most work?

2. How would you rate your emotional bond or closeness with your child?

3. What do you do daily/weekly to create two-way conversations with your child?

4. Describe any family routines or rituals you have that help develop emotional closeness with your child.

5. Which of the three parenting styles best describes you? What about your spouse? Can you think of any specific ways you can tweak your style to make it better?

CHAPTER 5

Equipping Your Child for the Race—Discipleship (TRAIN)

Train up a child in the way he should go; even
when he is old he will not depart from it . . .
—Proverbs 22:6 ESV

One of the gold nuggets in Scripture that I believe presents parents a comprehensive curriculum guide is in Luke 2:52: "And Jesus grew in wisdom and stature, and in favor with God and man" (NIV). I am often asked what type of curriculum should be used to disciple and train our children. My simple response is to use Luke 2:52 as the curriculum guardrails every day. This frustrates parents. Everyone wants a book or some type of "how to" resource. Don't get me wrong; I have used many books and resources to help me gain insight and wisdom. There is a plethora of incredible material available that I highly recommend. However, I am suggesting perhaps a paradigm shift for most parents. Discipleship that elevates how Jesus trained His team—He taught by doing life with His disciples and observing and modeling for them. The four areas of growth for Jesus present a holistic plan of what we should be observing in our children.

Are your children growing in wisdom, stature, favor with God and with man?

This is where the concept of synergy plays a vital role in your child developing into a Christ follower, creating daily, weekly, and annual practices that allow you to observe your child in these four areas. First, let's establish a simple definition of these four areas and then we will visit specific practices that allow parents to guide and mentor their children.

And Jesus grew in wisdom: God's opinion on all knowledge; application of biblical principles to all areas of life

And Jesus grew in stature: Physical growth; spiritual wellness; emotional balance

And Jesus grew in favor with God: Personal relationship with God; Christ-likeness; obedience; passion; love for our Savior

And Jesus grew in favor with man: Personal relationship with other people; social skills; character traits; having a good name

How do we know if our children are growing in these areas? By talking to them, observing them, listening to them, and asking them questions. We support their growing in these areas by channeling them to people who are like-minded and who are also endeavoring to mentor children in these areas. These areas are observable and can be viewed in every facet of a child's life—especially during the informal times of life. The key for a parent is to be intentional in this observational process. It is these intentional practices that create the synergy, and it is the synergy that helps our children internalize the core values and biblical principles we desire.

Building the character of Christ into my child

This simple visual reminds us of the three components of our child's spiritual development. The house symbolizes a child's life and the components that build a strong foundation. Notice the foundation—the Word of God. There is no use beginning the building process of our child's heart unless we are committed to God's Word as the foundational source of all truth and wisdom. The four pillars anchored and supported by the foundation and holding up the structure of our child's character are the posterity pillars based on Luke 2:52. For example, the posterity pillar wisdom has to be built on the foundation of God's Word or else the prevalent human wisdom and empty philosophy will form the child's thinking and values. Finally, notice the protecting cover or structure for our child's character—it is these practices that complete a child's development. The family practices of communication, emotional closeness, parenting style and dealing with conflict represent "doing life" together.

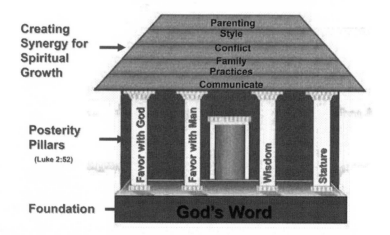

What core values and biblical principles should we desire? What should we pray for and what constitutes a discipleship plan for our children? Luke 2:52 provides insight for us in that our training plan for our children must be holistic. I want to introduce you to a training plan that is practical and seamlessly fits into everyday life. More importantly, it begins to connect the synergy-producing practices discussed in the last chapter to your daily, weekly, and annual schedule. It provides the substance to the four Luke 2:52 "posterity pillars." It is the glue to the discipleship of your children. In other words, the five areas comprising the **TRAIN**ing model provide the day-to-day focus areas that happen as you "do life" with your child. It is a merging of synergy-producing practices, posterity pillars, and the ultimate desired outcomes for your child.

*The **TRAIN**ing process happens throughout the day — it is how our Master mentored His disciples.*

I think you will see that these five areas, integrated into the soul, heart, and mind of a child, constitute a disciple of Christ. I have come up with an acrostic to help make the TRAINing model easy to remember:

> **T**ranscendent Purpose
> **R**everence for God
> **A**iming Arrows by a "3-D" Discipline Strategy
> **I**nternal Strength, Balance & Resolve
> **N**ecessary Life Practices

The "T" in TRAIN—Transcendent Purpose

While we are "doing life" with our children, we want to model, instruct, and pray that our children seek a transcendent purpose and that they fully understand God's "big picture" perspective. There is something and someone bigger than we are. God has a purpose and a plan that is far more important than anything we could do or accomplish on our own. A global view helps our children understand the difference between the temporal and the eternal (2 Corinthians 4:18). It is God's agenda that we pursue and seek—it is not about me.

We emphasize by word, deed, and lifestyle that:

- The greatest honor here on earth is to serve as His ambassador.
- We perform for an audience of One.
- There is absolute Truth and God's Word can be trusted, believed, and obeyed.
- We are to seek His agenda and move people on to it (Blackaby).

What does this look like on a day-to-day basis? How is this applied? The simple and most fundamental answer is that this **TRAIN**ing component is better "caught than taught." It is in the parents' living this out and not just talking about it. The child has to see Mom and Dad (and ideally teachers, pastors, and peers) consistently and authentically modeling that God is first and everything derives its purpose and order through that priority.

How is this "caught?"

- By consistently seeking God in prayer
- By consistently seeking truth and wisdom through the study of His Word
- By consistently asking God where He wants you to serve and then doing it
- By consistently putting others first and serving them unconditionally
- By consistently investing your resources (time, talent, and treasure) into Kingdom-advancing people and projects, developing the "big picture" perspective

Children must see us using our financial capital to meet the needs of others and for projects that advance the Kingdom

A successful businessman and friend of mine, Kent Sterchi, felt God calling him into ministry. I admired Kent and watched him make this transition into a ministry that focused on the discipleship of men. Delinda and I prayed about financially supporting Kent and, although our annual gift was not significant, it still represented our total support and belief in Kent's ministry. For several years I would pull the Taylor boys together when I wrote the check and mailed it to Kent. We would pray for him, and I explained to our sons what Kent was doing and how he was being obedient to God. It was a simple opportunity to illustrate the importance of supporting Kingdom projects—the transcendent purpose.

Introducing our children to local needs

Family night out—feeding the homeless

When I was a high school principal at The First Academy in Orlando, Florida, our guidance counselor and campus chaplain, Steve Kavanagh, started meeting some high school students at the Orlando Public Library on Saturday nights—not to read, but to feed the homeless people. I kept hearing great things about our students so I decided to join them—with Delinda and the boys in tow. The boys were nine, seven, five, and three at the time, and when I first told Delinda where we were going, there was silence. I will never forget that first Saturday night. I was the only one who got out of the van. But after a few trips, the whole family was joining the high school students and me as we ministered to the hundreds of homeless men, women, and even children. One of my fondest memories was pouring hot coffee into Styrofoam cups that Chas (my three-year-old) was holding. Looking back on it, I realize it probably wasn't very wise for me to let my preschooler help hold cups with HOT coffee. However, I knew that God had done some powerful things in the hearts of my sons when at our evening prayer time, the boys started praying for their new homeless friends by name.

Children must see the world beyond our home and city

I believe mission trips provide one of the greatest opportunities for spiritual development. For several years, I have been traveling to Cuba to work with some key Christian leaders who are truly making a difference for the cause of Christ. As my boys entered high school, I began taking them with me. The most effective sermon on the Great Commission (Matthew 28:19-20) was getting my boys out of the comfy pews and classrooms and onto the mission field. By seeing the houses or shacks where the people lived, they learned to be grateful. By sharing their faith and leading people to Christ, they learned to be bold and confident. By serving others through painting or yard work or other projects involving manual labor, my sons learned the importance of sharing Jesus through the less glamorous acts of love.

Mission trips and service-oriented activities touch on more aspects of spiritual disciplines, biblical principles, and the exercising of one's faith than anything I have ever experienced. It takes the theory out of Christianity and authenticates it for your child. They witness things that simply cannot be created at church or in your living room. It is a practice that connects and highlights the other **TRAIN**ing points discussed in this chapter—but especially the Transcendent purpose and cause. Our children see firsthand the tremendous needs of others and the responsibility we have as Christians to serve them and feed them with physical and spiritual food. I have personally witnessed this with my four sons and with many other children.

The "R" in TRAIN—Reverence for God

While we are "doing life" with our children, we want to model, instruct, and pray that they develop a deep reverence, respect, and love for the Lord. I often tell parents that if I could only choose one of the five areas in the **TRAIN**ing model, this is the one I would emphasize. It is the fundamental condition of a person's heart and the foundation for respect and honor. This will serve as the inner moral compass as our child goes through life. Without a genuine fear of the Lord, nothing else in the Christian life really makes sense. Again, we emphasize by word, deed and lifestyle that:

- We serve a Holy God.
- We understand that our sin hurts our heavenly Father and we must be reconciled to Him.
- We are to "guard our heart because out of the heart comes the wellspring of life" (Proverbs 4:23).
- The fear of the Lord is the beginning of wisdom (Proverbs 1:7).

Over 800 times in the Bible the reference to heart and reverence is made. This is such a foreign principle to this secular culture in which our children are growing up. Respect, honor, and reverence for anything, much less our Almighty God, is rare. Sad to say, this has even permeated the walls of the church. What does reverence look like on a day-to-day basis? How is this applied? Once again, the simple and most fundamental answer is that this **TRAIN**ing component is better "caught than taught." Our children need to observe us consistently and authentically treating God with reverence and honor.

How is this "caught?"

- By consistently demonstrating reverence while praying
- By consistently demonstrating reverence during church worship
- By consistently modeling reverence when reading and studying God's Word
- By consistently directing the child's sin toward the condition of his heart (emphasizing that good or poor behavior, emotions, and thoughts are connected to his heart)
- By consistently expressing gratefulness for God's grace, mercy, unconditional love, and forgiveness of sin

It is important to note that preparing the soil of our child's heart is crucial for the seed-planting process throughout the child's life. I like how Ted Tripp explains this in his book *Shepherding a Child's Heart*:

> *Therefore, your parenting goal cannot simply be well-behaved children . . . your concern is to unmask your child's sin, helping him/her to understand how it reflects a heart that has strayed. That leads to the cross of Christ. It underscores a need for a Savior.*

The "A" in TRAIN—Aiming Arrows by a "3-D" Discipline Strategy

While we are "doing life" with our children, we want to implement a biblically-based discipline model. Psalm 127 describes our children as being like arrows. When I think of an arrow I think of sharpness, balance, and direction—all three characteristics are important for an arrow to be purposeful. The same is true for our children. They must be sharp in their discernment and decision-making; emotionally and spiritually balanced in their approach to life's highs and lows; and live their life purposefully and with direction. I believe the Bible is clear that parents are responsible for aiming or directing the arrows with which they have been entrusted.

I love my boys, but they came out of the womb looking for trouble. The need for us to discipline our children is inevitable. The real question is whether or not we will do it in a biblical manner. It should not surprise us that the mainstream philosophy and practices for disciplining our children are very secular and not biblically sound. Unfortunately, this includes many opinions from Christian circles—they have substituted biblical principles with man-centered practices.

Aiming our arrows, or children, requires a biblical model of disciplining that I call a "3-D" approach:

Biblical Discipline = Discipline + Discernment + Direction

It is important to emphasize that all three Ds need to be implemented each time a child is disciplined. Too often parents only hear about discipline during parent training courses without any emphasis on discernment and direction. True biblical discipline results in our child becoming more discerning as well as more directional in making good choices.

We emphasize this **TRAIN**ing component by:

- Understanding that all three Ds need to be applied in order for purposeful discipline and discipleship to take place
- Understanding that proper discipline leads to discernment and provides direction
- Understanding that the intangible tool for success as a Christian is being able to discern based on biblical truth and principles
- Understanding that bringing children to maturity requires proper discipline
- Understanding the reasons for using the "rod" (or spanking our children) and how to discipline without the use of the rod
- Understanding the biblical principle that discipline is sorrowful for the moment (Hebrews 12:11-12)

We see in Scripture the importance of developing discernment—Hebrews 5:14

"But the solid food is for the mature, and because of practice they were able to discern good from evil . . ." The point is that discernment is needed in order to choose between good and evil, right and wrong, good and bad. I view the word "practice" as an opportunity to coach our children throughout their many good and bad choices in life. We see in Ephesians 6:4 another scriptural rationale for disciplining our children—" . . . but bring them up in the admonition of the Lord . . ." The Greek word for "bring them up" is *ektropho,* which means to *rear up to maturity.* Once again we are encouraged to proactively and purposefully raise our children to a point of maturity.

But what does maturity actually look like? I would suggest that maturity has three components, which are connected back to the Luke 2:52 maturity paradigm. What does this look like on a day-to-day basis? How is this applied? This is not a simple black and white response. There are hundreds of scenarios that require a parent to discipline a child, and each changes somewhat depending on the child's age. Although it is impossible to cover every situation, I can offer some universal principles and helpful suggestions. And, let me encourage you a little, this is the number-one request from parents during my Kingdom Family training course—we all are challenged in this area.

How is biblical discipline administered?

- By consistently separating a child's behavior into one of two categories—a willfully disobedient act or a thoughtless disobedient act

  o If it is willful disobedience, the use of the rod needs to be considered
  o If it is thoughtless disobedience (not willful or defiant; a careless or impulsive choice), the creation of a consequence that relates to the poor choice should be considered

- By consistently demonstrating a calm, under control, and empathetic reaction (compared to anger and out of control behavior)
- By consistently allowing your children to own the consequences of their choices

The broken ceiling tile

During one of the holidays, I went up to the church's sports and fitness center. I took three of the boys with me and while I was working out in the weight room, Luke, Zeke, and Chas were tossing the football in the lobby. Luke was ten, Zeke was eight, and Chas was six. Soon after I had started my workout, the boys walked in and confessed to breaking a ceiling tile with the football. I wasn't too happy, and the first thing I had to do was decide whether this was a willful act of disobedience (purposely destroying property) or a careless and thoughtless act (not willful or intentional). I determined it was a careless act, which took the rod option off the table; however, there was still property damage.

Ironically, the director of our Sports and Fitness Center lived in my neighborhood. So I called Joe and told him what had happened and that I was going to bring the boys to his house so they could report the damage, apologize, and ask how much it would cost to fix it. I specifically requested of Joe that he not let my boys off too easily and to understand this was an opportunity for training. You should have seen their eyes when we stopped in front of Joe's house. They nervously knocked on the door, and when Joe opened it, they "made restitution"—they apologized, asked for forgiveness, and found out how much they owed to fix the ceiling. The bottom line is that my boys needed to own the consequence of their behavior. The easiest thing for me to do would have been to call Joe myself and ask how much we owed. But I would have lost a great opportunity to coach my kids.

The crayon artwork on the classroom floor

When Luke was in kindergarten, he decided to draw some pictures on the tile floor using crayons. The teacher handled it perfectly and communicated to us what the consequence was going to be. Luke was going to have to make an appointment with the school custodian, confess what he had done, and ask for a bucket of soapy water and a sponge. With the teacher by his side, Luke did meet with the custodian and apologize. Twenty minutes later, Luke was finished scrubbing the floor. Again, my son owned the consequence of his behavior. It is also important to note how important it was for Luke to be in a school where we as parents were of the same mind as the teachers and working together on training my child. Your children spend eight to twelve hours a day at school (if they are not home schooled) and there are plenty of opportunities for character building moments during this time. When the home and school are on the same page, our children are receiving a congruent message, which, of course, is an essential element in training our children.

The act of disciplining a child, especially when using the rod, is one of the most difficult things for a parent

It is an understatement that disciplining our children is one of the most difficult acts for a parent. However, aiming the arrows requires an authoritative parent style (love blended with strict firmness). It is very clear in God's Word that parents should discipline their children and, in fact, that this is an expression of love. What makes this even more difficult is how differently God wired each child. Dr. Dobson categorizes children as either strong-willed or compliant. The strong-willed child typically lets you know what is on his mind. The compliant child also has things on his mind; he just usually keeps it inside. Regardless of the child's temperament, when a willful disobedient act is done, the rod needs to be considered. I am very concerned with the contemporary views of discipline in mainstream culture and the strong discouragement of using the rod. Unfortunately this philosophy has crept into the church.

If God's Word is what you rely on as absolute truth, then it is disobedient for a parent not to use the rod: "Whoever spares the rod hates his son, but he who loves him is diligent to discipline him" (Proverbs 13:24 ESV). "The rod and reproof give wisdom, but a child left to himself brings shame to his mother" (Proverbs 29:15 ESV). "Correct thy son, and he shall give thee rest; he shall give delight unto thy soul" (Proverbs 29:17 (KJV).

Suggestions for when to use the rod

I recommend using a literal rod (not your hand or the belt). A small wooden spatula-type instrument is an effective discipline tool. The three-step process when spanking (using the rod) is:

1. Point out to your child precisely why he or she is being disciplined (make sure he recognizes his sin); do this in private and not in an angry voice.
2. Spank your child just below the buttocks two to three times, enough for a painful sting but certainly not with an amount of force that injures or creates bruises or welts.
3. At some point, restore the child by hugging, holding, and telling your child that you love him or her; at times this will naturally take place right after the spanking and other times it will be later, but it is crucial that this happens before going to bed that evening.

There are a variety of opinions on what the specific age should be when use of the rod is discontinued. Generally, most agree that the natural time to cease using the rod is when a child is in middle school (before entering high school), and has gone through puberty.

The "I" in TRAIN—Internal Strength, Balance, and Resolve

While we are "doing life" with our children, we want to allow God to use trials and tribulations to mold, mature, and grow our children. We cannot see what He sees, and we have to trust that His purpose and plan for our children requires God-ordained difficult seasons in life. God's Word is very clear that challenges and difficulties are His method of training, teaching, and growing us to maturity in Him. C.S. Lewis calls "men without chests" those who have failed to develop the internal character that helps guide one through all of life. There are two biblical passages that I would encourage you to meditate on and pray through regarding the development of your child's inner character and resolve: "Consider it pure joy, my brothers and sisters, whenever you face trials of many kinds, because you know that the testing of your faith produces perseverance" (James 1:2-3 NIV). "In all this you greatly rejoice, though now for a little while you may have had to suffer grief in all kinds of trials. These have come so that the proven genuineness of your faith—of greater worth than gold, which perishes even though refined by fire—may result in praise, glory and honor when Jesus Christ is revealed" (1 Peter 1:6-7 NIV).

We emphasize this **TRAIN**ing component by:

- Trusting that trials will enhance our children's spiritual foundation

- Allowing children to go through a "healthy" level of anxiety and not stealing an opportunity for God to work in their lives; this will challenge all parents but especially the permissive parenting style, or "helicopter" parents who hover over the child and, as soon as there is anxiety, swoop in and "save" the child
- Praying for patience and endurance through the often agonizing moments of watching a child go through a trial
- Inserting my child's name in the James 1:2-3 and 1 Peter 1:6-7 Scripture passages and personalizing God's Truth with my family and situation

How are internal strength, balance, and resolve administered?

- By consistently praying and seeking God's understanding every time I sense the need to intervene during one of my child's trials
- By consistently encouraging children to finish whatever commitment they made (a sport season; a project at school or home; a class at school; a chore; etc.); it should never be easy to quit
- By consistently encouraging and guiding your child to deal with people (a teacher, coach, sibling, or boss) face to face when going through a difficult time or problem
- By consistently creating opportunities for developing responsibility

Early in our parenting journey, I received incredible practical advice for developing children to be responsible (a core component to maturity) from Dr. Bob Barnes. I highly recommend everything Dr. Barnes has written; he has had more influence on my parenting than any one person. Below are some steps from Dr. Barnes regarding practical ways of training our children to be more responsible:

- Provide an opportunity or task.
- Provide proper training for the task.
- Provide clear expectations and deadlines.
- Allow the expectations and deadlines to be owned by the child (do not constantly remind him).
- Allow the rewards and consequences of failure to teach and guide the child.

Taylor "weed-pulling parties"

For several years I had the boys help me with the outside chores—the entry-level work I titled the "weed-pulling party". I started the boys pulling weeds when they were preschoolers. I used the weeds to do a lot of observing, evaluating, and teaching. I observed their work ethic and their attention to excellence. I evaluated their "whine-tolerance": How long it took them to start whining about the heat or about their brothers. I taught them the proper way to pull a weed—all weed-pulling experts will tell you that you have to get the whole root or else the weed will grow back quickly. One lesson that was particularly important to me dealt with the weeds that were behind the shrubs and totally out of sight. We knew about those hidden weeds, and leaving them there would not be right; the task would be incomplete. The boys struggled with that lesson, but I knew it was a principle worth drilling down. Years later, when Bryce was in high school, we were celebrating Christmas and Delinda handed me the last present to be opened. It was a poem from Bryce. I got special permission to put the poem in this book, but notice his comment about the weeds—I was blessed beyond words. Stay committed to the small things, parents, even if you are not sure your children are learning what you want them to learn.

The Man
By Bryce Alan Taylor

There was a child went forth,
and from Tradewinds Trail to Gaston Foster—
from Austin Way to Big River—
he continued to go forth every day.
watching that man called "Daddy,"
whose traits and habits and gestures, whose
    beliefs and words and attitudes,
whose very soul,
became a part of that little boy.

In those glorious summer days upon the
    mountain,
at the "Bwue Widge Assembwy,"
the summer haven of that little boy's family, to
    which they still yearly go—
the first climb up the mountain was
    triumphant,
the man leading the little boy, the little boy
    emulating the man,
and the sweat, the struggle, the celebration at
    the mountaintop,
were a part of that little boy thereafter.

Saturday was Doughnut Day for the man and
    the child, and the brothers of the
child,
glazed, sprinkled—
white, pink, chocolate icing—
the soft and sugary texture of seemingly
    limitless round treats—

these were pleasurable for the child.
But in the midst of such lip-smacking pleasure,
    the child watched the man,
soaking up the very character of the man
who showed love, showed concern toward the
    doughnut people,
toward the other doughnut eaters, and the
    coffee drinkers, and the newspaper readers,
but especially toward the little boys at the
    man's table,
including the child, who absorbed the love and
    care displayed in the man.

And on those scorching days, when the weeds
    were at their highest,
when the grass reached halfway up the boy's
    shins,
the boy's spirits would sink into sorrow at the
    assault of the enemy—
the rays of the sun, the bite of the ants, the dirt
    of the flowerbed.
But the man, shiny with sweat, would spur him on,
demonstrating the discipline that gradually
    imbued itself upon the character of the boy,
and teaching the boy to pull the weed from the
    root,
and to pull the weeds behind the bushes, the
    weeds that nobody would ever see,
teaching the boy that the outward show was
    not what mattered,
but rather what you did when nobody would
    see.
The boy learned this, and carried on with the
    dreadful weed-pulling.

The boy became a young man, and played
    football as the man once had.
It was not his prime pursuit, but he continued
    in it,
thoroughly enjoying each victory and success,
the grandest being the state championship,
at which the young man's team achieved the
    ultimate triumph of the sport,
and in which the young man twice scored.
And afterward, in the midst of victory, the
    young man found the man,
whom he embraced in smiling joy,
and who told the young man he was proud of
    him,
a comment so profound, not for its lack of prior
    use, but for its elated sincerity.
And the young man felt love and warmth so
    real as to be nearly touchable,
and he was moved by it.

These became part of the child who went forth
    every day, and who now goes, and will
    always go forth every day.

The "N" in TRAIN—Necessary Life Practices

While we are "doing life" with our children, we want to model and train them in the basic spiritual disciplines and the fundamental biblical principles of adulthood. These spiritual disciplines and adulthood principles are meant to perpetuate lifelong habits that nurture one's spiritual journey as well as one's future family and role within a local body, or church. In essence, they are necessary to develop a steadfast and self-disciplined commitment to Christ and to be an active participant and leader in your child's future family, work, and church.

Although it is never too late to train your children on these disciplines and principles (we adults are still learning these), I would strongly suggest you begin most of these as early as age two or three (I will provide specific suggestions later). Disciplines and principles are internalized because of years and years of parent-modeled examples and the child being encouraged, motivated, coached, and held accountable to be a participant. Of course, the goal is that your child becomes genuinely engaged with these disciplines and principles and not just compliant to your expectations.

The most important training point of these necessary life practices is to connect them to the other **TRAIN**ing components. In other words, we train our children to pray, study the Bible, and be an active participant in church so that they begin to earnestly desire and seek His agenda and transcendent purpose for their lives (the **T**) and so that they begin to revere, love, and respect their Lord (the **R**) and to develop direction, discernment, and wisdom for all of life's endeavors (the **A**), and we train our children to work and to manage their finances in order to diligently prepare for God's assignment (work) and mate (family), knowing that our internal strength, character, and resolve will be needed to sustain a lifelong service for the Lord (the **I**). It is these necessary life practices (the **N**) that guide our children to the finish line.

What is the finish line? Remember Psalm 78? Specifically verse six, ". . . and even the children yet to be born." The finish line is the great baton of faith hand-off for our grandchildren. As I mentioned earlier, in essence, we are not training children, we are training child-raisers. It is these necessary life practices that will not only sustain our children for their lives, but that will be the foundation for them as they train their children and lead their families.

We emphasize this **TRAIN**ing component by:

- Modeling these disciplines and principles to our children
- Developing an annual personal, marriage, and family plan so that these disciplines and principles are deliberately monitored for the purpose of growth and continuity (this annual plan will be discussed in detail in chapter six)

What does this look like on a day-to-day basis? How is this applied?

- By consistently providing parent-led prayer time; Bible reading time; and family devotions/discussions (with the goal of transitioning to child-led; parents decrease and the child increases as they get older; the goal is that they "own" these disciplines and principles before they go to the university)
- By consistently maintaining a strong commitment to church attendance and involvement
- By consistently praying for and participating in service and mission-oriented activities
- By consistently emphasizing biblical stewardship of talents, time and treasures and providing guidance on tithing and investing in Kingdom projects
- By consistently looking for and planning opportunities for family traditions
- By consistently planning for children to participate in work around the house and ultimately a job outside of the home

Some day you will be providing for your family

Go find a job

Our deal with the boys was that they had to get a job at least two of the four years in high school. I relaxed on that expectation during their varsity football or basketball season due to the strenuous schedule, but after the season they had to find a job. As much as I wanted to make a phone call and get the job for them, I restrained myself, knowing that part of the life lesson was the journey of applying and interviewing. Six applications later, Bryce (the first Taylor guinea pig at finding a job) landed a job at a Jamba Juice. I will never forget his first day on the job. He came home and told us about a lady who pulled up and parked illegally in the handicapped spot (in her convertible Mercedes). She proceeded to order her drink, and Bryce didn't quite have the cash register skills down pat so he was slow and messed it up. Well, the lady lit into him and gave him a piece of her mind. Delinda felt sorry for Bryce, but I was high-fiving him saying, "Welcome to the real world, Bud."

Luke, our second child, landed a job as a waiter at Steak-n-Shake, and we visited him on his opening night. Everything was going well at first since we were one of only three families in the restaurant. But a mad rush of people came in and Luke was running around taking orders and smiling. The only problem is that we were not getting any attention from our waiter—Luke. Finally he came over, and with a look of desperation on his face, he asked, "Is it okay to not take your order so that I can get to the other customers?" He was scrambling, and we were happy to wait for our food—we even left him a great tip! He learned a lot about people, working with different supervisors and fellow employees and creating his overall work ethic principles.

Zeke, our third son, and Chas, our youngest have both gone through the same process. Zeke landed a job at Wingstop (great wings!) and Chas at Chick-fil-A. There is something about having to report to a boss; being trained and evaluated; and going through the learning curve where you are not naturally proficient at something (like learning the drive-through cash register at peak time during lunch hour!). The trials, successes, and growth that your children experience while working for someone else are training opportunities. When children begin generating revenue, it also opens the door to a variety of stewardship and money management training possibilities.

Money does not grow on a tree, guys— you have to pay the bills

One of the most productive exercises I did with the boys was pulling them all in for our annual family budgeting routine. Delinda and I showed them all of the budget categories and how much money we spent on each one. The boys were absolutely blown away at how much money it took for the house, utilities, cars, gas, insurance, and so on. I didn't feel the real impact of this training until the next time we went out to dinner. First of all, two of the boys didn't even want to go out because they wanted to save the money. When I finally convinced them that it was okay to enjoy a night out, they all jumped on me for ordering a Diet Coke—"Dad, do you know how much money you could be saving by just drinking water?" It was one of the best stewardship activities we ever did.

Final comments

I hope this TRAINing device helps you see the balanced approach to raising your child. As I have said before, these five areas are meant to be implemented as you "do life" with your child. Consistency is the key. Your child will grow and mature in wisdom, stature, and favor with God and with man.

Chapter 5 Application

1. The four Posterity Pillars, based on Luke 2:52, provide a daily curriculum for parents to follow as they disciple their children. What are some practical ways that you can apply each one as you raise your children?

2. The "T" for "Transcendent Cause" encourages us to train our children to see the "big picture" of Christianity. What are some personal examples where you are modeling this for your children?

3. The "R" stands for "Reverence;" what are some practical ways you can teach your children to be reverent? What specific circumstances or situations require reverence?

4. The "A" is for "Aiming the Arrow" through biblical discipline. The 3-D approach focuses on Discipline, Discernment, and Direction when it comes to disciplining our children. What are some non-negotiable offenses for the use of the rod and some appropriate consequences for non-rod situations?

5. The "I" represents the "Internal Resolve and Strength." What are some trials that your child has experienced that have provided opportunities for growth?

6. The "N" is for the "Necessary Life Practices" that should be the focus of the training of our children. Think about habits or characteristics you want to see in your child when he/she is twenty-two to twenty-five and list some ways to develop those specific traits or behaviors.

CHAPTER 6

Developing a Family Plan

We will not hide them from their descendants; we will
tell the next generation the praiseworthy deeds of the
LORD, his power, and the wonders he has done.
—Psalm 78:4 NIV

When I served as high school principal at The First Academy in Orlando, Florida, I required our teachers to turn in their lesson plans by Friday afternoon. These lesson plans told me what each teacher was planning to do with their students the following week. They stated their curriculum objectives and how they were going to present them to the students. Every Monday morning I would remind the teachers who did not turn in their lesson plans on Friday by slipping a note on yellow paper into their teacher mailboxes. These plans were important to me, and they were a quality control parameter that helped us maintain the highest standards in our learning environment—the bottom line was that I did not want our teachers to "wing it" in the classroom.

On one particular Monday morning as I slipped a few yellow reminders in some teacher mailboxes, I heard a whisper in my ear: "Larry, where is your lesson plan?" I froze. It was as if God was standing beside me asking me a series of questions. "What is your plan today with your sons? When you go home today, Larry, to the most important classroom you will visit, what is your game plan to mentor and disciple your boys? What about your marriage, Larry? Do you have a plan today to strengthen your marriage? And, Larry, what about your personal spiritual development plan? What is your plan to grow in your relationship with Me?"

I stood there, stunned. I expected more out of a high school teacher than I did out of myself. I had no plan. I was going through the typical motions—prayers before meals and at night and church on Sunday and Wednesday. A deep conviction pierced my soul that day. I would never want our math teacher to show up for class without a very specific plan, and yet weeks and months were going by and that was exactly what I was doing. I would never have walked into my basketball practices without every minute of my two-hour practice clearly planned out, but I was plan-less with my parenting, marriage, and my own spiritual life.

I spent more time developing my annual budget and vacation plan than I did developing a spiritual growth plan for my family—something had to change.

Through this ordeal, I spent months and even years seeking God's heart on this issue. I spent time with godly men, seeking their counsel. I began to transition to a more intentional mindset as it related to my shepherding responsibilities with my family. I began developing a weekly plan for my personal spiritual life, my marriage, and for the spiritual development of my children. I started noticing that I was not alone and that many parents were going through their parenting simply winging it. My personal journey, alongside my observations of many other parents, compelled me to begin spending time with other parents for the specific purpose of developing an annual family plan—a plan that was more deliberate. I realize that the following suggestions might seem ultra-structured and more mechanical in nature compared to simply being relationship-oriented.

The Kingdom Family Plan

Requires the development of three annual growth plans:

1. A personal spiritual development plan
2. A marriage (or preparation for marriage) plan
3. A family, child-discipleship plan

I believe it is fundamental to develop and operate these three plans simultaneously. Although these three areas represent distinct components and should be analyzed that way, it is imperative to accept the fact that all three are interdependent. Countless times, I have seen incredible dads who have built a wonderful relationship with their child only to find their marriage dead. I often see parents who are deeply committed to growing their personal lives, characterized by weekly Bible studies with men's or women's groups, only to find that they have a horrible relationship with their spouse or child. These three plans work together—an organism with every part crucial for the survival of the family. Imagine a football coach who separated his defensive coordinator from the offensive coordinator from the special teams coordinator all of the time. Certainly, these three areas of the team have to have their own game plan, but the great coaches know that they are interdependent and need to work within the context of a cohesive and unified team game plan.

The goal is that your children do not know you are on a plan until the right time. The key to this multi-year plan is that it is natural and fluid. What I mean by natural is that it fits into your everyday life and that it does not come across as robotic and structured. When the children are young, this is not a problem but as they get older they will become more observant and skeptical if they sense a structured plan. What is the right time to pull them in and let them know you are on a plan? Every child and family is a little different, but my suggested guidelines are twofold.

First, one of the ultimate goals, remember, is that you are not just training your children, you are training your grandchildren—Psalm 78: ". . . even the children yet to be born." This emphasizes the importance of training our children on why a plan is important and how to set one up. Second, as soon as you feel your child is mature enough to begin participating in setting up their own personal spiritual development plan, this is precisely when I would pull them in. With our four boys, we began pulling them in during their middle school years. They not only began developing their own spiritual development plans for the year, they also were part of helping me set up our overall family plan. During this time, I shared with them that my prayer was to someday receive a phone call from them telling me that they had just finished their Bible time and prayer with their son or daughter. This would be the Psalm 78 principle coming full circle.

The Kingdom Family Plan requires a complete three-part plan to be developed once a year (similar to reviewing and adopting an annual financial budget except this is an annual Kingdom Family Plan).

1. The plan should be evaluated midyear
2. The plan should be printed out (I keep mine in a three-ring binder)
3. The plan should have daily, weekly, and annual goals for each of the three parts comprising the Kingdom Family Plan

The Kingdom Family Plan requires a weekly "staff meeting" with Mom and Dad (for single parents I would recommend this is done with a close friend—accountability partner) to discuss:

1. Parenting plan you adopted and published (what is working and what is not working; adjustments you need to make)
2. Calendar for the week (to discuss schedules or if any adjustments need to be made for the week)
3. A simple "touch-point" to discuss any special challenges or blessings that have come up that week; this could be marriage-related or child-oriented
4. Prayer needs for the children or anything related to the family plan

Defining the Kingdom Family Plan objectives

You should select a good time and place to work on your annual plan. Delinda and I started setting aside the last week of June to work on our plan. Why? This is when we attended an annual family conference in North Carolina. As I said previously, we have attended this family conference for twenty-seven straight years, primarily because it meets two of our annual goals for our family plan—a marriage conference and a family conference. We needed to get away from the fast pace of life in order to slow our minds and hearts down. I especially needed this slower pace, and being in the beautiful Blue Ridge Mountains served us well. Regardless of when and where, the key is to develop an annual routine so you will be able to have the time and the right atmosphere to reflect and plan.

Larry Taylor, Ph.D.

The importance of daily, weekly, and annual goals

Most parents recognize the long-term goal of producing godly offspring. I have never had a parent tell me that his or her desire for children was anything less than being a follower of Christ throughout their lifetime. The problem is not the long term, but the short term. Busy days turn into busy weeks, which turn into busy months. Before you realize it, a year has gone by and then two or three years. An annual plan needs to be broken down into weekly goals, and weekly goals need some daily direction. I believe this is where the traction begins. This is where children begin to notice patterns, priorities, and principles—this is authentic discipleship. Jesus did not take his team out on a retreat once a year—it was daily. Everyone in the family needs daily goals for their personal spiritual development plan. Every marriage needs daily and weekly goals to keep the intimacy going. And every family needs some daily and weekly goals that keep the parent/child relationship focused and intentional.

Identify the midyear point of your annual plan and calendar it

Right around Christmas and New Year's Eve was the perfect midyear point for us. We call this "half time." Great coaches win ball games during half time, and I believe the same is true for parents. We need a time where we can reflect on the first half of our family plan to see what is going well and what adjustments are needed. I always joke with families that they don't want to hang around the Taylors during New Year's Eve—we just got accustomed to using this as our midyear reflection. Over the years, these reflection times have resulted in minor tweaks to the family plan and occasionally a major overhaul.

The important thing is that you remain honest and open about your plan and what adjustments you need to make, if any.

Pick the best time every week for your staff meeting

Don't laugh. Yes, I want to encourage you to find a weekly time to meet and discuss your plan. I call this the staff meeting because I have always wondered why we don't think twice about having staff meetings at work but never have them at home. We meet at work to review goals, objectives, projects, budget, and for strategic planning. Why not do the same for the most important project of our lives—our family plan? Delinda and I found that Sunday night was the best time of the week to huddle up. The busy whitewater rapids during the week seemed to slow down to a calmer flowing river on this night.

Sometimes our weekly meetings lasted five minutes and sometimes fifty minutes. I would say that our average meeting time was around fifteen to twenty minutes. I believe these meetings are crucial. If I were the enemy coaching against you, especially if you were becoming intentional on passing on your faith to your children, I would get you so busy that months would go by before you realized how far off you were from your plan. Then I would make you feel so guilty that you would want to give up—of course the result would be your not wanting to do it again the following year. Great coaches begin every week with a well thought-out plan—they look back to reflect on what has transpired the past week and they look forward to make sure they are on top of executing what they have set out to accomplish. This prevents parent-coaches from winging it and the intentionality becomes a blessing as you see consistency. The key to the family plan is gaining traction through ritual and routine.

Consider printing out your plan for accountability purposes

I know you are probably thinking that I am a structured control freak—not at all. I want to encourage you to print out your overall family plan for one purpose—accountability. The power of accountability is real, and it serves as a major force for momentum. We all need it. For years, my "printed-out" plan was simply some hand-written notes tucked into a three-ring binder. I had sections for all three plans (personal, marriage, and child discipleship), but other than that it was pretty basic. Some parents have spiced their plan up a bit, but it really does not matter—as long as you like it and it is readable!

Accountability is scary. I had no idea at first where the accountability would go, and I was surprised along the way, but I can assure you that I needed it. The initial impact came from my wife. Once I took that first step in actually showing her some of the specific ideas, it was now officially out of the bag—she knew about it, and it scared me. I did not want to disappoint her. Then, when my children became accustomed to our daily and weekly goals (even before I started pulling them in to help me set up the plan), they really kicked the accountability up a notch. Have you ever had a five year old remind you that it was "Bible and prayer time"? They are like piranhas on a pork chop—wow, I never had better accountability partners than my own children.

The third example of accountability was when I started to share my family plan with some very close friends, or accountability partners. For a few years I had two men who were privy to my family plan and I to their plans. When these two men saw me, they just didn't say, "How is the family, Larry?" They said, "How is your weekly discipleship meeting going with Zeke (one of my sons)?" This specificity became a layer of accountability that helped me remain true to the plan.

Step by Step Process to Building Your Kingdom Family Plan

Step One—Personal Spiritual Development Plans

Everything rests on this plan. How can a marriage grow or a child be discipled without a parent deepening his or her walk with the Lord? Remember the biblical principle of Luke 6:40—your children will most likely look like you. The personal plan requires some integrity as you inspect your life. This is an excellent opportunity to integrate the spiritual disciplines discussed in Chapter 5 under Necessary Life Practices. For young children, parents actually set up the personal plan in order to begin the spiritual disciplines training that someday they will own. I would suggest the following template for a well-balanced personal plan.

Daily

- The reading of God's Word, and as this progresses, the studying, meditation, and memorization of biblical truths and principles.
- Fellowship with the Lord through prayer so that on a regular basis you are expressing your adoration, thanksgiving, and gratefulness to Him. You are also confessing sin and claiming I John 1:9. You are presenting requests to your heavenly Father and you are praying for your children, marriage and overall personal direction for your life.

Weekly

- Reading and studying some component of a worldview area (usually a book). Some type of specialized training in a worldview area such as in the sciences (origin of man—evolutionary contradictions with Scripture; atheism—arguments that God does not exist). Although there is no replacement for God's Word, it is amazing how many additional resources are available that help us understand the biblical application. It is also amazing to see how many books one can read throughout a year just by having a weekly goal and routine of reading.

Annually

- Two to three books a year that deal with biblical doctrine or a book in the Bible or a worldview area.
- Consider a course or two at church or online that deals with biblical doctrine, a book in the Bible, or a worldview area.
- Consider a conference that provides training in any area of spiritual enrichment or worldview area.

Step Two—Marriage (or preparation for marriage) Development Plan

I will never forget being with my bride at a marriage conference early in our pilgrimage—I believe we had been married for five or six years. The conference speaker guided us through the love languages exercise and asked each spouse to circle his or her top three love languages. I noticed that Delinda had only selected one and pointed that out to her, thinking she had not understood the directions. In a very gentle yet direct way, my sweet bride softly said, "Every time we do this exercise I mention my top love languages, and I have told you for four straight years that my number one love language is affirmation—all I need is for you to affirm me." At that point she took the pencil and circled the word affirmation—I got the point. I knew I needed extra help in this area since it was not natural for me to affirm her—or anyone, for that matter. Guess what my daily goal was that year—you guessed it, to affirm my wife at least three times a day.

Daily

- Consider a daily prayer time or even a joint devotion from God's Word (could coincide with the personal plan).
- A reflection time on the day to talk and establish routine communication.
- Any personal needs that have been identified, such as my example of wanting to affirm Delinda on a daily basis.

Weekly

- Consider a date night and enjoy dinner or visit a coffee shop.
- Continue to regularly plan or discuss times of intimacy.
- Consider a brief discussion on what you are learning or what God is teaching you as a result of your personal spiritual development plan.
- Consider merging some of the above into your weekly "staff meeting."

Annually

- Consider a joint Bible study or a book reading.
- I highly recommend a marriage conference every year. This sounds relatively easy, but it takes planning and budgeting. Delinda and I have attended a marriage conference every year of our twenty-seven years of marriage—we call it our "annual tune-up." I think this

has had more impact on our overall family plan than anything else!

- Consider playing the "V-Game," or the vulnerability game. For years, every New Year's Eve, Delinda and I would set aside an hour and answer two questions. What two or three things had each of us done in the past twelve months that had been positive and an overall blessing for each other?—that was the fun part. The difficult part was the second question—what two or three things did each of us fall short on and what did we need to focus on over the next twelve months? Wow, there were some tough moments playing that game, but it kept us growing and honestly reflecting on our relationship—I highly recommend this "game."

Step Three—Child Discipleship Plan

You have the two foundational plans flowing, your personal and marriage plans. I believe that the child discipleship plan draws from this reservoir of personal and marriage healthiness. I want to remind you how important it is to keep this plan fluid and natural. Remember your "curriculum" cues, discussed earlier, from the Luke 2:52 principle. Let these four areas serve as a constant guide to how you intentionally observe your children and how you deliberately set up a discipleship plan for them. Remember your end goal—the Acts 17 disciple. If you want your children to have these qualities when they are older, begin presenting these principles early and reinforcing them along the way. And don't forget the **TRAIN**ing paradigm; use these five areas to make sure you are providing a "balanced" training diet.

And the main thing—keep it simple and base the plan primarily on principles. For example, I wanted my four sons to know that God's Word was pre-eminent; and to be used to a deeper level of understanding and critical thinking (running with the horses); and to be grounded in the spiritual disciplines and life practices. Of course, all of this looks different with a three-year-old compared to a thirteen- or seventeen-year-old; however, the principles of all three of these are universal in nature and can be applied developmentally regardless of the age (including into adulthood!).

Daily

- To read God's Word; when our sons were two, three, and four, this came in the form of a picture Bible and was part of the evening bed time routine (Dad, this is an excellent opportunity to build in some daily time with your children); as your children begin to learn to read, let them take over the Bible time and simply guide them with questions (excellent opportunity to transition to deeper level critical thinking questions as they get older); as your children reach the age of nine, ten, and older, begin introducing a "quiet time" concept where the evening Bible time is directly connected to their individual Scripture reading (you are now focusing on a spiritual discipline that they begin to own and your daily and weekly accountability is key).
- As your children get older, consider studying a book of the Bible together and use the evening time to discuss and share.
- On average we accomplished this goal four out of the seven nights, sometimes more often and sometimes less; however, often enough that this became routine and "expected;" when I was out of town traveling, we would connect over the phone. Delinda would put me on speaker phone and we would have a brief Bible and prayer time with the children.

- Prayer time; daily prayer time can certainly take place in a variety of ways—morning through bed time; I would encourage you to integrate this time naturally into the same time you do Bible time.

I believe the single most important thing we did with our boys was our daily Bible and prayer time—God's Word became routinely discussed, honored, and prioritized. Discussions around biblical truth became regular, and critical thinking about application developed as the boys got older.

Weekly

- Weekly worship and church related programs (such as Wednesday night children and youth programs) are essential and fundamentally important.
- A family activity that becomes a ritual, such as game night or ice cream night; for over ten years straight every Saturday morning, as I mentioned earlier in the book, I would take the boys to Dunkin' Donuts—I usually started this when the boys reached two years old; my only goals were to have fun, build a positive relationship, and to communicate that spending time with them was important to me (Delinda loved having the morning off!).

Annually
- I highly recommend an annual family conference; as mentioned previously, we have attended the same family conference for twenty-seven years and the children look forward to it every year (even as they transitioned into college).

- Look for opportunities to do service-oriented activities together as a family and even mission trips together (earlier I shared about our family feeding the homeless).
- Some of my fondest memories have been taking my boys and Delinda with me on mission trips to Cuba (I mentioned this earlier; however, I don't think one has to go on an expensive international trip; there are plenty of opportunities in our community, city, and state).
- Consider reading a book or two with your children and integrate the discussions into your evening Bible and prayer time.

One-on-one discipleship time

- My goal with each child was to spend some extra time with them (one-on-one) between the ages of ten and twelve. Typically, this precedes the river of hormones that begins to mature our kids into young adults. During this two-year period, I would meet two to three times a month for around an hour or so. This is when I would focus on some of the basic manhood issues (or womanhood, if you have a daughter), character, integrity, and Christlikeness.
- During this two-year period I would take two special trips with the child I was focusing on at that time; these trips were typically part of a business trip I was already scheduled to go on; this really spiced up this focused discipleship time and provided something for the child to look forward to; it communicated that they were important to me, and it took our relationship deeper.

Sample Plan

Here is a sample Taylor Kingdom Family Plan from several years ago. I prettied it up for you since my handwriting is so messy! It includes a personal plan for all six in our family and then the master family plan. I also included a suggested multi-year discipleship-family plan that shows you exactly what we did with our boys when they were two to five years old, five to eight years old, eight to ten years old, ten to twelve years old, and twelve and older. The only reason I am providing this sample is that I have been asked hundreds of times by parents to see an example so that they can get a better understanding of what I am talking about. In no way do I want to come across as "look at me and my family plan." I hope this helps you as you begin working on your plan.

Sample Family Plan

Taylor Family Plan

2001 Taylor Family Plan	Dad	Mom	Bryce 13 yrs. old	Luke 11 yrs. old	Zeke 9 yrs. old	Chas 7 yrs. old
Daily	**Personal** • Quiet Time • Bible Study **Marriage** • Prayer Together • Connection/Talk • Affirm Delinda 3 times **Child(ren)** • Evening Bible & Prayer Time	**Personal** • Quiet Time • Bible Study **Marriage** • Prayer Together • Connection/Talk **Child(ren)** • Reinforce Focus Area	**Personal** • Quiet Time • Bible Study • Evening Follow-up With Dad & Prayer **Family** • Play time (sports, wrestling, etc.)	**Personal** • Quiet Time • Bible Study • Evening Follow-up With Dad & Prayer **Family** • Play time (sports, wrestling, etc.)	**Personal** • Bible Time • Evening Reading With Dad & Prayer • Begin Quiet Time **Family** • Play time (sports, wrestling, etc.)	**Personal** • Bible Time • Evening Reading With Dad & Prayer **Family** • Play time (sports, wrestling, etc.)
Weekly	**Personal** • Sunday Church • Begin Wednesday teaching/class • "Staff" meeting **Marriage** • Date Night **Child(ren)** • Saturday Donut Shop	**Personal** • Sunday Church • Women's Bible Study • "Staff" meeting **Marriage** • Date Night **Child(ren)** • Reinforce Focus Area	**Personal** • Sunday Church • Wednesday Youth Group • Choir **Family** • Saturday Donut Shop/Dad	**Personal** • Sunday Church • Wednesday AWANA • Bible Drill • Discipleship Program/Dad **Family** • Saturday Donut Shop/Dad	**Personal** • Sunday Church • Wednesday AWANA • Bible Drill **Family** • Saturday Donut Shop/Dad	**Personal** • Sunday Church • Wednesday AWANA **Family** • Saturday Donut Shop/Dad
Annual	**Personal** • Read 1-2 books on worldview topic **Marriage** • Attend Marriage Conference • "Vulnerability Game" **Child(ren)** • Book study with Bryce • Discipleship w/Luke-special trip • Attend Family Conference • Mid-Year Family Plan Evaluation-Adjustments	**Personal** • Read several books • Participate in Bible studies **Marriage** • Attend Marriage Conference • "Vulnerability Game" **Child(ren)** • Attend Family Conference • Mid-Year Family Plan Evaluation-Adjustments	**Personal** • Read book with Dad • Attend FCA sports camp • Attend Church Youth camp **Family** • Attend Family Conference	**Personal** • Discipleship program • Special trip with Dad **Family** • Attend Family Conference	**Personal** • Review 3-4 books of the Bible with Dad **Family** • Attend Family Conference	**Personal** • Review 3-4 books of the Bible with Dad **Family** • Attend Family Conference
Special Focus Area	1.**Prayer:** Pray every day for a different group (family, missionaries); become "other-centered" 2.**Missions:** Begin exploring a family mission trip 3.**Family:** Local Services; Feeding the homeless		4.**Tithing & Overall Giving:** train kids 5.**Special Times:** Ranger games, camping trips 6. **Update Family Manual:** Design the weekly "staff" meeting format and template			

The plan below is what we focused on as our children grew older and matured. I hope you see the basic commitments and yet the consistency around these basics, such as the focus on God's Word.

<u>2-5 Years Old</u>

- Introduce the Bible and God.
- Engage in daily Bible reading.
- Become familiar with facts and people.
- Introduce basic Biblical principles.

<u>6-8 Years Old</u>

- Continue daily Bible reading.
- Elevate expectations of facts such as "people of the Bible."

Elevate critical thinking questions/discussions such as, "Why did Jesus die?"

<u>9-10 Years Old</u>

- Introduce personal quiet time (the daily Bible time goes to the next level . . . transitioning into a lifestyle practice/habit).
- Evening discussions take critical thinking to another level . . . With questions such as, "How does this relate to you?"
- Introduce responsibility at church . . . note-taking, comprehensive discussions about church/school.
- Continue principles . . . kindness, giving, work, family, modesty, friends who are equally yoked, thinking on wholesome things—music, movies, reading.

11-12 Years Old

- Continue personal quiet time and evening sessions . . . establish your children as true accountability partners (another lifestyle practice/habit).
- Continue engaging children in critical thinking questions.
- Continue emphasis on church responsibility.
- Introduce a "Discipleship Program" . . . a one-on-one program whose ultimate goal is to finish before the hormones hit!

13 Years Old and Beyond

- Continue personal quiet time and evening sessions.
- Continue church responsibility.
- Focus on mentoring/coaching . . . a transition from discipleship training.
- Introduce special topics and studies on finance, marriage, time management based on biblical principles, work through special books together such as *Living Above the Level of Mediocrity*.
- Introduce special ceremonies.

Final Thoughts

I want to invite you to dive into developing your own family plan. My guess is that you are already doing most of what I suggested. Perhaps a few small tweaks will make it even more intentional. One of the intangibles about the Family Plan was that it truly provided guardrails to help me, and us, stay on track. With daily and weekly goals, we alleviated the problem of busyness taking over. Within a few days or weeks, we could tell if we were getting out of balance as a family, as individuals, or in our marriage. We would run into the daily and weekly routine guardrails if we were steering off the road, mainly due to this necessary accountability.

Chapter 6 Application

1. Have you ever sensed that you were winging it as a parent? What are some ways you can be intentional in your parenting?

2. Of the three components to a kingdom family plan (personal, marriage, and child), which one is easiest for you? Which one is your weakest area?

3. When would be an ideal time every year to work on your family plan? What about a midyear review?

4. Take some time to consider daily, weekly, and annual goals or objectives for each of the three components. Write down your ideas and then discuss them with your spouse or accountability partner.

5. When would be a good weekly time for a staff meeting with your spouse or accountability partner?

PART 3

Developing Depth in Your Child's Faith

So then, just as you received Christ Jesus as Lord, continue to live your lives in him, rooted and built up in him, strengthened in the faith as you were taught, and overflowing with thankfulness. See to it that no one takes you captive through hollow and deceptive philosophy, which depends on human tradition and the elemental spiritual forces of this world rather than on Christ.
—Colossians 2:6-8 NIV

CHAPTER 7

Checking Perspective

*...being confident of this, that he who began a good work in you
will carry it on to completion until the day of Christ Jesus.*
—Philippians 1:6 NIV

It was the end of the school year, and I was facilitating our faculty meeting where we were selecting some of the student awards. We had clear criteria to help us through the selection process, but there was one huge problem—our faculty was having a hard time nominating students. We discussed several students, but we ended the meeting with no selections. I picked this up again a week later at our next faculty meeting. I began to smell the aroma of negativity in the air, and as the second meeting concluded with still no students being nominated for several character-based awards, I knew we were in trouble. At the next faculty meeting, I opened up by asking one of our teachers what he did as a hobby during his high school years. I already knew the answer because I had interviewed, hired, and gotten pretty close to him over the span of a few years. He told the faculty that he played in a heavy metal rock-n-roll band. I went to the next teacher and the next. It only took four teachers before they knew what I was up to. I smiled and reminded them (and myself) that they were not perfect in high school either—we selected several students for character awards that day, and we were proud of each student.

I call this the "Billy Graham Syndrome"—in honor of one of my heroes. It is a common obstacle for parents in that if their son or daughter is not the next "Billy Graham" by ninth grade, we think the world is going to end. Certainly we have failed if our tenth-grade child does not wake up every Sunday morning excited about going to church. And if our eleventh-grader is not consistently having a devotional time in God's Word, he or she is destined to become an atheist. Well, I certainly do not want to make light of some very important spiritual disciplines and character traits—not at all. However, I think we all need to be reminded that the transformation occurring within the hearts of our children is not on a school calendar timeline. Of course we want to see the fruit of an Acts 17 disciple before they head off to the university, but it is natural and normal for the spiritual maturation process to continue well into the college years and into adulthood. It never really ends, does it?

There is an unhealthy pressure within the Christian community that sometimes impacts how we parent our kids through trials and tribulations. This also carries over into how we feel about ourselves, often feeling like failures if our child has made a poor choice: gets caught cheating on a test at school; gets benched at the ball game for poor sportsmanship (witnessed by all); makes a poor choice at the weekend party; does not like the music standards you desire; wants to read some novels that are on the edge; the list goes on. All of the eyes are on you, right? You can almost hear the other parents talking about you and questioning what in the world you did wrong that led to your child doing such a thing. Let's admit it, I think it is pride. I am not talking about the genuine pain we feel when our child is breaking our heart over some poor choices. I am referring to the "I don't want anyone to think that I am a bad parent" type of pride.

We all need a perspective check.

Remember, Jesus was thirty when He started His ministry. Yes, thirty! We get down on our kids and ourselves when our child is not perfect by Graduation Day—and Jesus started at thirty. The purpose of this book is to challenge you to be intentional as you disciple and **TRAIN** your children, and now I am encouraging you to be patient. You are not the heart changer—Jesus is. You are not the Holy Spirit. We need to be diligent, consistent, and deliberate as we mentor our children, but we also need to recognize and accept that we cannot force the maturity cycle to fit into our desired timeline.

I have to remind myself that even up to the final hours before Christ was to be crucified, He was still noticing that His students needed some more work. Do you remember the scene—Jesus taking a basin of water and a towel and washing the feet of His disciples (John 13:5)? Jesus had spent three long years with this group, and they still did not get it. This is the Master, our Lord and King, and He still had trouble after investing His heart into these men. Do you remember how Jesus sought Peter out after the crucifixion and resurrection? He cooked breakfast for Peter on the beach and restored Peter's shattered spirit after he had denied his Lord three times. Countless other times Jesus rebuked Peter for his poor choices, actions, or attitude. Peter became one of the greatest evangelists of all time. The other disciples died for their Lord. We need to be patient parents and provide unconditional love for our kids—the same love Jesus provided for Peter and the other disciples—the same love Jesus provides for you and me. His grace, mercy, and forgiveness for you and me are reminders that we need on a regular basis as parents.

But notice what Jesus was doing when He was in middle school. In Luke 2, we see Jesus at the local arcade playing games—wrong! He was sitting with the wise men in the synagogue. He was listening and conversing and basically amazing the older men with His wisdom and knowledge. Although we may expect too much out of our children, as I mentioned earlier, we also may fall prey to expecting too little. We simply have allowed a spirit of mediocrity and low expectations to become mainstream in our homes and in our churches. There is no doubt in my mind that our children can and will do more, grow more, and be more than what is generally the norm today. The bottom line is that we must let the Holy Spirit be our guide as we guide our children.

Have you ever had a seventh-grader hold you accountable? Jennifer Albert Dukes (now a happily married pastor's wife with six precious children) was undoubtedly one of the godliest young ladies in our school. She loved the Lord and lived for Him in every way. In the midst of the turbulent middle school years, she truly separated herself from the typical issues facing this age group. Her identity was in Christ and she was secure—she did not need the world's temporary fixes. Bill and Kathleen Albert, her parents, are dear friends and they raised their children by modeling Christ, intentionally **TRAIN**ing them and building a very close relationship with them. Jennifer and I decided to hold each other accountable for our daily quiet time—yes, a seventh-grade girl. Every day we would ask each other whether or not we had spent time in God's Word. I have to admit that there were several days I tried to avoid her when I had not had my quiet time—it stings to look bad in front of a seventh grader! Middle school students can be more than what we expect of them. Thank you, Jennifer, for helping me grow in my faith.

Have you been invited to join them on their playground lately?

The reality is that as our kids get older, there is a "playground" transition that naturally takes place. When they are young, they insist that you join them on their "playground"—the place they love to play and have fun. You don't have a choice but to join them playing in the backyard, building blocks, or wrestling—they don't take no for an answer. It doesn't matter that you are wiped out from a long day at work or have chores around the house. As time goes by, those invitations decrease. In fact, there are those stages when our children do not want us near their "playground." It is tough to go through those phases, but it is part of the maturity process. What is my point?

Two things—maximize the early years (usually up to age thirteen) and be more intentional in the later years (usually ages thirteen to eighteen). The experiences on their playground are limited, so take advantage of them—don't miss them. This is where the emotional closeness with your children is cultivated. An intentional family plan is crucial during this phase of parenting because it will establish proper work hours, daily routines, and weekly fun experiences. Trust me, the weekly visits to Dunkin' Donuts eventually started to decrease as the boys got older. But when they were young, it was a simple and inexpensive way to be on their "playground." The research shows a typical pattern that creates a tug-of-war between work and parenting during the early years. Most parents are having children at the exact time their career is the most demanding. The hours at work are not as flexible, and climbing the corporate ladder is intense during this time. It is a true battle and one that I understand. Even more reason to have a family plan that will discipline you not to miss the most important part of your day—spending time with your family.

Remember, you have 6,570 days from birth to diploma—no amount of money or power can change this amount of time with your children.

As the busyness of the middle and high school years hits, life changes in many ways. The most pronounced impact on the family plan is simply finding the time to maintain routine. For us, it became more difficult to have dinner together, read the Bible and pray in the evenings, and continue the weekly visits to the doughnut shop. Schoolwork, sports, church programs, and other activities began to take over our family time. Again, even more reason to have a family plan—or the busyness of individual schedules will take over like a tsunami. Be realistic and maintain a proper perspective. Delinda and I determined that it was okay to adjust our family plan so that it aligned with the different seasons of life. It was okay and even good to integrate some of the unique aspects that sports and other co-curricular activities introduce. We found that maintaining the frequency of dinners together, evening Bible and prayer sessions, and special fun times was still doable—but we had to work at it.

I want to deal specifically with one of the greatest challenges to our family plan and one that I hear about all of the time—select sports, fine arts involvement, academic load, and church programs for youth.

How do you balance it all? Let me warn you, I used to be a varsity coach and now oversee a school full of varsity coaches—there is no one more committed to developing an athletic and arts program of excellence than I am. I want to hang state championship banners and would never want to compromise what it takes to get there. I am on staff at a church, so I have a perspective from this side as well, knowing that the opportunities churches provide are very important for the development of our children.

With that said, I believe that something has to be the rudder of the ship—the family ship.

If you are not careful, the ship can be going full steam in too many directions, wreaking havoc on the family. More often than not, the god of sports becomes superior to the family and church. I do not think this is healthy, biblical, or ever the right thing. However, I do think there is a proper balance that can be maintained. Family and church must become the top two priorities and everything else secondary. Although it is not easy, this balance can be established without totally losing the competitive edge and preparation that is gained from involvement in a select program. All four of my sons were competitive athletes, and we have firsthand experience playing year-round select sports. They also were involved in varsity athletics while maintaining a rigorous academic load. Finding a balance was not easy, and we were not always successful, but we did learn some helpful tips along the way.

First point of advice: develop your family plan and conform the select program around it regardless of the cost. The family plan should include the daily, weekly, and annual spiritual development goals for each person in the family. There should be some non-negotiable standards that are established, such as not missing church on a regular basis. Remember the **N** in **TRAIN**ing—Necessary Life Practices, where church and family were a recommended lifelong core value. What message are you sending to your children if they miss church on a regular basis in order to make the select baseball or soccer tournament? Remember my premise—that there should be one superior rudder directing the family ship. I do not believe it should be the sports rudder. What is the proper balance?

Be "selective" of the select program

My boys consistently played on year-round select programs (primarily basketball and some baseball). We intentionally did not join programs that traveled around the state or country. We were still committed to highly competitive tournaments and were okay with having to miss church occasionally as long as it did not become habitual.

Make sure the coach is okay with your parameters before you join or try out for the team.

When one of my boys was asked to join a premier select baseball team in Florida, I spent two hours on the phone with the coach. First of all, I wanted the coach to know where we were spiritually and that church was a priority for us. I also wanted to know where the coach was spiritually, knowing full well that my son would be spending a lot of time with him and the culture he created. We came to an agreement that my son would most likely not make the first game of the Sunday double-headers because of church. The coach was okay with that, but I also had to be okay with the coach's position that this would definitely affect my son's playing time and overall status on the team. And it definitely did! On occasion, our son (and other sons) missed church altogether, but again, this was the exception and not the rule. We were able to make those difficult decisions because our family plan established our priorities and helped us determine the best options for our sons. Obviously, there were times our priorities were out of whack, but it usually didn't take long before we painfully bumped into the guardrails that had been established.

What if my son or daughter is a top one-percent athlete?

I am specifically referring to those athletes who are clearly ranked by credible amateur organizations related to Olympic or other similar status groups. In other words, they are not the ones in the "wannabe" group, which is where most of our children will be (including my boys) but truly on another level of competitiveness. Well, I would still say, what is your superior rudder? I just cannot endorse anything that would hinder the establishment of your child's spiritual and family foundation. I have worked with families and athletes who are in this category, and although it takes work, it can be done. The guardrails might look different for every family, but the safety net that is put in place is the most important thing.

Back to the select baseball team that I referenced earlier— we were playing baseball year-round but also playing the seasonal sports such as football in the fall, basketball in the winter, and baseball in the spring. Before we realized it, the select baseball program dominated our lives. For an entire year, one son controlled our calendar. Nearly every weekend, we were driving all over the state of Florida. The schedule not only became unrealistic for church, it also became unfair to our other boys—it was creating a dysfunctional family unit. It was the last time we had a son on that level of select sports. What is your superior rudder?

What about school sports, academics, arts, or any co-curricular activity? And what about church programs including weekly events and annual summer camps and mission trips?

I am certain to make some coaches and pastors upset with my opinion. Let me use our personal example to navigate through this one. I had to tell many varsity coaches and youth pastors that my son was going to be attending our family conference—which meant they would miss summer games, workouts, church camps, and mission trips. At first, it was tough to do this, but I knew I was doing the right thing. Our family conference was part of our annual family plan—a key component to the spiritual development plan. Yes, my boys would have benefited from attending the workouts or the church mission trips—but there was nothing more important to us than this family conference. In other words, the school sports programs and the church plans did not dictate and govern our family plan. My boys went on plenty of church-related trips and camps, and they are better men for it—however, the church and sports plan had to fit into our family plan, not the other way around.

When my sons were in high school, they attended the Summit Ministries Worldview conference for two weeks in the summer. Although they did indeed miss their varsity workouts and their church camps while they were gone, this was part of our family plan and we determined that our boys were going to attend the conference. For our family, we knew that the training that Summit provided was critical when it came to preparing our boys for the worldview clashes they would soon have in college. Sadly, there are very few youth pastors providing training for students for the challenges they will soon face in college. I am not advocating quitting church, and I do not think that this is an example of "forsaking the assembly!" When I stand before God, I will be held accountable for the training and discipleship of my children—which includes being part of a church. However, when the church does not provide the level of training essential for my children to "run with the horses," then I will most certainly select the deeper level of training. To my earlier point and the major claims of this book, we need to change the training paradigm for our children. I wish more parents would tell their pastor and youth pastor that they have limited funds and limited days in the summer and that they need more than just another retreat with a great speaker and band—again, these retreats are important and needed. But you are the head coach of your family, and if you feel your child needs a deeper level of training and the church is not providing it, you have a responsibility to prepare your child for the battle that lies ahead.

I will close this chapter with one final perspective check:

I walked into my bedroom late one night ready to hit the sack. Delinda had long since retired for the night, or so I thought. I knew that this was two hours past Delinda's normal bedtime—and trust me, my wife treasures her sleep! Much to my surprise, I walked in to find Bryce lying there talking away with Delinda. We were just a few months away from dropping our first child at the doorsteps of a university dorm. Delinda wanted to go to bed, but she knew that Bryce wanted to talk— it was a time-out that she took advantage of and used wisely. When I coached, I quickly realized how valuable time-outs were because they were limited and could be game-changers. As our kids get older, we need to be ready for those special time-outs when they want to talk—no doubt they will not be during your most desired times. Nonetheless, they are special, few, productive, and ordained—use them wisely.

Chapter 7 Application

1. Do you struggle with parental pride? Does it bother you when others look at you when your child disobeys or makes a poor choice? What do you think is the best way to deal with the pride?

2. Do you have a balanced perspective of your child? Do you expect too little or too much from him or her?

3. Is there any activity that routinely alters your family plan (school, church, select sports, etc.)? Come up with some ways to help determine what should take priority and how to protect your family plan.

CHAPTER 8

Calling an Audible

But in your hearts revere Christ as Lord. Always be prepared to give an answer to everyone who asks you to give the reason for the hope that you have. But do this with gentleness and respect...
—1 Peter 3:15 NIV

One of my all-time favorite quarterbacks is Peyton Manning. Ironically, it is not his physical talents that I respect the most. That is saying a lot because I don't think there has been anyone with better physical skills. It is his intelligence and ability to make quick decisions under extreme pressure that is amazing. Because of Peyton's physical and mental abilities, he has won a lot of games, including a Super Bowl, and has set many records. I especially like when Peyton calls an audible at the line of scrimmage—no one does it better than he does. His knowledge of the game allows him to read the defense and determine the play in only seconds—his audible is usually very accurate. What a lot of people don't know is how many extra hours Peyton puts in studying films, meeting with coaches and players, and just talking strategy. He not only knows the details of his offense and the strengths of his players, he also understands everything about his opponent.

We need to be "Peyton Manning parents."

We need to know our game-book (the Bible) so well that we can explain it to our players (our children). We need to understand our opponent so that we do not fall prey to empty deceit or philosophy as Paul instructed us in Colossians 2:6-8. The Bible clearly points out that there is a real enemy who is seeking to devour us like a lion (1 Peter 5:8) and who is scheming against us (2 Corinthians 2:11). We need to be able to go to the line of scrimmage of life and call an audible. This is where parenting gets really challenging—but not impossible. What separates Peyton from other quarterbacks is his prep time (okay, and he is just downright good!). And what separates very good parents from Super Bowl-level parents is—prep time.

It takes time to know the Bible and sound doctrine, truth, principles, and worldview application. And what about our opponent? Do we study the culture and the empty philosophy of ideas that so easily entangle our children? It takes an investment of heart and a sacrificial commitment to read books, articles, attend conferences, and ask people questions. I have been convicted over and over of how lazy I am as a parent—just not willing to put in the prep time. Without sufficient prep time, we allow others to coach our kids, instead of doing it ourselves. We don't ask them the proper questions because we don't feel confident to discuss them. What I have discovered about me is that if I am not confident about a subject, I do one of two things—I either open my mouth and embarrass myself, or I retreat from the conversation and remain silent. Neither is good, obviously.

Is it possible that the impact of Christians on the culture has declined because we don't enter the discussions where important ideology is formed? Is it possible that we are not invited to the dialogue table where mainstream issues are debated because all of our arguments are based on the Bible which is not accepted as truth by many in today's culture? More specifically, is it possible that the root of this problem is centered in the home where parents don't tackle the key issues with their children? I believe so. Our homes need to be like

Peyton Manning's prep routine—wrestling with the important principles and ideas. We need our children to be confident when they enter the university and the game of life. They need to be eating "solid food" as it says in Hebrews 5:14.

If I were coaching against you (and trust me, the second greatest coach of all time—Satan—has a full-court press against you and your family), I would attack your confidence. I would attempt to make you fearful to enter a conversation with your child . . . a conversation about anything, especially about the Bible or worldview issues. A family without discussions rarely will grow deeper in its faith. This is especially true as our kids get older. As parents, we need to be ready for questions and be able to guide conversations with our children using biblical truth and principles. We need to prepare for the issues of life that our kids will certainly go through and be confident when we speak—everyone has opinions, but our words need to be God's opinion.

Do you remember when the world watched Terri Schiavo dying in her Florida hospital bed while the courts went back and forth on the legality of keeping her alive on life support machines? It captured the attention of the world. At the time, Bryce was about sixteen. We were watching a special report on the Schiavo case when his questions came—"So, Dad, what does God's Word say about this? What are we supposed to believe about this as Christians?" I was speechless. I think I made some excuse about having to use the bathroom so that I wouldn't embarrass myself. Bryce was way past the point of simply accepting the "sanctity of life" answer. He needed a deeper answer, one that required some time and study. I had to admit to him that I really needed to spend more time looking into this issue and that we should do it together. I knew the sanctity of life response, but he was looking for more.

I was at the line of scrimmage with Bryce, and the clock was ticking. I went from being a simple couch potato watching the news to having to be an audible-ready dad. My son asked a deep worldview question, and my lack of prep time was quickly evident. The deeper we are, the better we will guide our family down the field of life. We may not score every time, but we will at least be on the field competing instead of silently watching from the sideline. Naturally, we cannot be experts on every issue that comes up, but we must be humble enough to admit when we don't have an answer yet willing to invest the time to learn. It is important to know what the key issues are and have some level of biblical knowledge. You also need to know who is qualified to assist you and partner with you in those areas where you don't feel as knowledgeable.

Here are my suggestions for partnerships and "assistant coaches" to help you with your team. Don't expect secular-based schools (public or private) to help you train your students to have a biblical worldview. In fact, expect the same fruit from them that they have delivered for a long time—a secularized Christianity. What I mean by secularized Christianity is that your child will have become a Christian and regularly attend church, but their views on worldview issues will typically not be biblically based; they will come from a secular bent. If your goal is for your children to have a biblical worldview, then who partners with you to train them is obviously crucial. Possible partnerships include ministries like Summit Ministries, home school associations, Christian schools, and your youth ministry.

If you choose a secular-based school system, my strong encouragement is to be extremely intentional in countering this training with very specific biblically-based worldview training. I am not talking about regular church programs where your child spends one to two hours a week. I am suggesting a specific curriculum with trained leaders, such as what Summit Ministries provides. Their curriculum can be integrated into a youth ministry setting, but it would require pastors and youth leaders to add additional time or adjust existing schedules in order to fit it in. Although there are a few youth leaders doing a great job in this area, too many are consumed by scheduling their seeker-based outreach services, which are important, but they just do not provide depth in training. And if you are considering a Christian school, look behind their curriculum curtain and staff training to make sure they are genuinely integrating biblical worldview concepts. Not all Christian schools emphasize training students in the Christian worldview.

In your personal spiritual development plan, be intentional about becoming deeper in both biblical truth and worldview application (preparing yourself and your kids on the opposing worldviews). I would encourage you to study the books of the Bible, their themes, primary points, and doctrine. Understand the Bible as the meta-narrative, the whole story, and not just bits and pieces. Become a student of the basic components of the Christian worldview and apologetics.

I have always recommended personal growth in five key areas: biblical literacy, spiritual disciplines, cultural apologetics, parenting/family, and passion/devotion (your personal passion for Christ). It requires reading, studying, attending conferences, and going on mission and service trips. In the Appendix, I have included some suggested reading and activities for each of these five areas.

You will not only notice your confidence level increasing, but you will also be modeling this to your children. We need Peyton Manning parents. Manning does not complete every pass or win every game—and neither will we be perfect parents. That is not my point at all. But, like Manning, we will enter each day with a plan, and calling an audible will be more natural and fluid. We will be directing our team to be forward-thinking and heading to the goal line that Christ has set before us, instead of sitting back paralyzed by fear of the oncoming defense (the world's challenges). We will enter our family training time much better prepared to lead our children and to prepare them to thrive in the thickets and run with the horses—for the glory of God.

There is another type of audible that pertains just to your family plan. My suggestion earlier in the book was for you to develop and print out your family plan. A quick review: the plan consists of a personal spiritual development plan (for each person in the family), a marriage plan (or a preparation for marriage), and child-discipleship plan. Each plan is to have daily, weekly, and annual goals. And at midyear of your plan you are to have a half time in order to evaluate how things are going. But what if things are not going well with your plan? Or, what if something is going very well or has the potential to go very well, but you don't have it in your plan—what should you do? Let me recommend two things for you to consider:

First, don't panic too soon and overhaul your plan. Give it some time. Great coaches always go into the game with a plan, but the first few minutes show how the theory part of the plan is actually going to play itself out. Family plans take time for everyone to get used to. Don't worry if things are not perfect the first few weeks. Getting into a daily and weekly routine takes a level of repetition before you can properly analyze and suggest changes. One of the reasons championship teams reach the highest possible levels is because they stick to a core set of fundamentals and they continue to do them until they perfect them. Work your plan long enough to give it a chance, and by all means do not overhaul your entire plan—stick to your core objectives and make minor adjustments . . . and practice, practice, practice!

Second, remember you are the head coach, and your job is to make adjustments. Yes, do not panic. However, you will always know your family better than anyone else. You will know your needs, your marriage needs, and the needs of your children. You will understand the circumstances surrounding your family and the most intricate details of your family dynamic. If you sense an adjustment needs to be made to any part of your family plan, then do it. Your plan should be somewhat flexible and fluid and should never turn into a legalistic document. Your instinct could be the Holy Spirit nudging you in a different direction. Great coaches don't wait until halftime to make all of the adjustments; they tweak their plan along the way as the game provides key feedback. The same should be true for parents—as you do life with your children, you may need to make some minor changes in order to get your family into a better flow which can create positive momentum and traction.

I had to make some "audibles" as our family grew. While our child count went from one to two to three to four, I found that the number of hours in a day did not increase. Bible and prayer time in the evenings with one child was manageable. We had a twenty- to thirty-minute bedtime routine. Then with our second child, the evening time turned into nearly an hour. I wanted to do the same thing with our second that I did with our first child. It started to get very difficult with our third child—the evening sessions stretched well over an hour. And then came our fourth child—for a few weeks I did four separate Bible and prayer times that stretched at times to two hours long. I would then come down the stairs and collapse. In fact, it was pretty common for Delinda to find me asleep in one of the boys' beds. I was trying to maintain a part of our plan that logistically was nearly impossible. I found myself cutting corners to save time, which really defeated the purpose.

My point in telling you this is that I had to make a change. I did not want to make a change because I had done the same bedtime routine for over five years with the boys. But it was just not working—I was starting to not look forward to Bible time and prayer with my boys! I told Delinda I was going to try something new, so I reduced the four evening sessions to two. One group was the older two and the other group, the younger two. This worked much better, and I started to get back to a more manageable schedule as well as a positive attitude. Eventually I reduced the two meetings down to one—and I really enjoyed this group setting. With this setting we were able to:

Build on the value of family—This presented excellent opportunities for the boys to pray for each other. They listened to each other read and discuss the Bible. It also allowed me to have some joint training time where I emphasized being reverent during Bible reading and prayer time. Don't get me wrong, we had plenty of non-spiritual moments where I could not resist a good wrestling match, but all in all this was a time for the Lord. This was not a perfect set-up. I remember when Bryce shared his frustration about having to do Bible time with his younger brothers and putting up with their immaturity. I told him that I totally understood, but that it was so important for them to see their older brother being a role model.

Have a joint Bible study—We would choose a book of the Bible and we would read and discuss a chapter or a few verses during our evening time together. I remember going through Romans, 1 & 2 Corinthians, Philippians, Ephesians, the Gospels, Proverbs, and more. I started encouraging the boys to read their Bible in the mornings so that we could go straight into the discussion at nighttime. I was training them to begin their personal quiet time.

Develop a personal quiet time—Then, one day our oldest asked me if he could read Psalms. At first I was resistant because I wanted to maintain the uniformity of the routine (everyone going through the same book of the Bible). One night, it hit me like a brick that this is precisely the type of request I should be desiring and approving: a child who is interested in exploring the Bible! I turned him loose on Psalms and then, one by one, the boys started reading a book of the Bible of their choice. The evening sessions turned into all of us reporting what God was showing us in our individual quiet times. There were many times when one or two of the boys had not done their quiet time. I tried not to react in a negative way when they had not done their Bible reading. I just encouraged them to try to remember to read their Bible the next day. If this became a pattern, I would pull them aside and talk to them about it privately. The bottom line was that I wanted this to become their own personal quiet time and not a mandate from me for them to just check off a list.

Have some great discussions and critical thinking time—I tried to use Bible time for inserting questions that would make the boys think and analyze. I wanted them to do more than just read and pray. I wanted them to think about how specific biblical truths could be applied to school, friends, sports, our family, their hearts, and every area of life.

The bottom line is that the family dynamic changes as the children grow and mature. Daily and weekly schedules change as they transition from elementary to middle to high school to college. The plan that worked during the elementary school years probably won't work when they get into middle and high school. Evening activities due to school, sports, and other hobbies change the dynamic. It is okay to make these adjustments—as long as your new plan still elevates your core fundamental values.

When the game of life turns your world upside down

I was facilitating a math department meeting when my assistant opened the door and calmly voiced a code word that meant I was needed immediately in the office. As we hurriedly walked to the office, she told me that my boss, Mr. Ed Gamble, The First Academy's headmaster, was on the phone and that it was an emergency. Mr. Gamble explained that Payne Stewart, celebrity golf pro, but more importantly a TFA dad, was in a life-threatening situation. Payne had boarded a private jet earlier in the day and was traveling to another state for a business meeting. The plane had malfunctioned and was now flying through the air out of control. Mr. Gamble then instructed me to get the Stewart children, Chelsea and Aaron, out of their classes because the news was all over the television and Mrs. Stewart did not want the kids to learn about this in a random way. At first, I thought Ed was joking—he and Payne were known for their pranks. He wasn't joking. It all started to make sense. I remembered Payne and his wife, Tracey, talking about the trip he was to take Monday morning while we watched our two boys playing in their Pop Warner football game over the weekend. Ed asked me to pull the kids in to my office and let them know what was going on—Tracey had a car on the way to bring the kids home. My heart felt like it hit my feet—I wanted to sit and cry. This was a nightmare unfolding.

I pulled Chelsea (eighth grade) and Aaron (fifth grade) into my office and carefully explained to them that the plane their daddy had boarded that morning had malfunctioned, and that we were not sure what was going to happen. Minutes later there was a knock on my door—I was told that the plane had crashed. I sat and held Chelsea and Aaron's hands and informed them that the plane had crashed and that most likely their daddy had died. We cried. The next few days and weeks were crazy—the world was shaken over this event.

Two things I remember most about this tragedy. When I visited the Stewart home a few hours after the plane had crashed, I will never forget what Tracey said as I hugged her— "Larry, I believe that Payne will actually have more impact for God through his death than if he were alive." She was right; I believe the whole world heard the gospel the day of his funeral—the golf channel piped it into every living room and golf course country club in the universe. A few weeks later, sweet Chelsea approached me in the hallway at school. She was carrying a small bag and she asked me if she could show me something. Out of the bag she pulled the WWJD (what would Jesus do) bracelet that Payne had been wearing when the plane went down. Everyone remembers Payne wearing this bracelet after he became a Christian—he wanted the world to know that he had surrendered his life to Christ. Chelsea looked in my eyes, smiled and said, "Can you believe this, Mr. Taylor? They actually found this bracelet at the accident scene!"—What a miracle!

Just a few weeks later our school was hosting a Date Night for fathers and daughters and mothers and sons. Chelsea stood before her friends, faculty, and school families and shared her heart. She said that although her daddy was supposed to be with her at this event, she trusted she would date her daddy some day in the future when she met him in heaven.

What is my point?

Tracey Stewart, wife and mom, had to call an audible. Her life changed in an instant. I watched this beautiful person walk her kids through one of life's most challenging valleys while she was grieving the loss of her husband. I was blown away at her selflessness, steadfast spirit, and the way she loved her precious children through the pain. There is no way an eighth-grade girl would be able to stand up and address the audience of her peers and their parents without her mom's support and love. Parents, sometimes we have to deal with changes that are way out of our control—they happen. The game of life brings many unplanned events—are you preparing to call an audible? Can you prepare for the unexpected?

Chapter 8 Application

1. Read Colossians 2:6-8. How do you feel this applies to your parenting practices? Share your thoughts.

2. What specific things are you doing to increase depth in your spiritual walk and worldview? What about for your children?

3. Evaluate the assistant coaches you allow to mentor/teach/coach your children. Are you comfortable with their worldviews? If they are not Christians, what are you doing to counter the secular influence?

4. List some challenges that you and your family have faced and how you were able to walk your children through the difficult times.

CHAPTER 9

Preparing for the University

Do your best to present yourself to God as one approved, a worker who has no need to be ashamed, rightly handling the word of truth.
−2 Timothy 2:15 ESV

I am amazed how quickly time flies. One day you are bringing your child home from the hospital, eager to raise him for the world's challenges, then the next you are moving him into his dorm room, away from the safety of your home. It is a very unique experience and one that covers the gamut of parental emotions. Is my child ready? Did I do everything I could do to prepare my child? Will my son maintain a vibrant faith and find a local church body to call home? How will our family adjust to my child being gone? These and many other questions flood your mind for several months. If the four years of high school have been used wisely, I think you can reduce the anxiety significantly. In addition to visiting college campuses and seeking God's will for the right college for your child, I want to suggest a few things for you to consider adding to your family plan during the four years of high school. If you still have a few years until the high school season, I still think it is important to look ahead and begin forming your game plan.

The primary focus during these four years should be on worldview issues. Regardless of the church or the type of school one is attending, I think deliberate Christian training is essential. Paralleling the focus on worldview is a concentration on what I call attitude. I think the attitude can be divided into two categories—an attitude of confidence, and an attitude of humility through servant-leadership. Finally, during these four years, one should pay close attention to church commitment and especially to the small group relationships and routines that are developing (or not developing). Of course, the normal daily, weekly, and overall family plan goals are continuing. I believe it is crucial to take advantage of these high school years, especially during the summers. Let me begin with the attitude.

The attitude

Can you imagine a great football coach repeatedly telling his players that their opponent was awesome and more talented and skilled than his team? That kind of coach would not survive long. No, great coaches know how important it is to develop the proper mindset and attitude. They know that regardless of how talented their opponent is, they must prepare their players to have a confident outlook. I think this is an area (preparing the attitude of high school students prior to college) on which the Christian community could improve.

Over and over again we hear how difficult it is to maintain faith, purity, and overall spiritual focus when in college. Additionally, we condition high school students to adopt a defeatist attitude by constantly referencing the normalcy of backsliding during the university years. I believe it is why so many Christians put God on the shelf for four years—they know that it is somewhat expected of them. We need to quit talking about compromise. We need to coach our children to have a positive attitude about the upcoming challenges of college. It IS possible to remain Christian in college!

Do we really believe that God is more powerful and victorious than any "thicket by the Jordan"? Indeed, the world poses some extremely challenging vices for our children, especially during the college years. However, the last time I checked Scripture, we win! Our God is bigger than any professor with two PhDs. Our God is bigger than the partying scene and purity challenges. Our God provides security, confidence, and purpose that establish authentic identity in Christ. There is nothing that can be thrown at our children that our God has not already faced and conquered. We can create scared children or confident soldiers for the Lord. Again, I understand the real obstacles our children will face while in college, and I am not trying to underestimate their potential for destruction. However, we need to hold true to the scriptural claims of "I can do all things through Christ who strengthens me" (Philippians 4:13 NKJV). Our children need to enter the university seeing it as an opportunity to be an ambassador for Christ.

I like how Jay Strack, founder of Student Leadership University, positions the proper attitude: "We have a simple goal at Student Leadership University—we just want to train students to change the world." My suggestion to help develop the correct attitude of your children is to make sure they hang around people like Jay Strack. Part of the family plan for our boys was for them to attend at least two years of Student Leadership University (SLU) for leadership and attitude training. There are a lot of Christian camps that students can attend during the summer months, but I can assure you that very few (if any) are as effective as SLU. While most Christian camps talk about the danger zones of college life, SLU focuses on succeeding and thriving in the secular universities.

I believe that practicing humility and being other-centered is critical in developing the proper attitude. There is a lot going on in the lives and minds of kids through their teenage years.

These can be some of the most difficult years for them and for parents. I believe they can also be some of the most rewarding as you begin to see some fruit from seeds planted a long time ago. One of the most challenging areas in training children is teaching them to be other-centered. As mentioned earlier in the book, one of the characteristics of an Acts 17 disciple is having the attitude and mind of Christ (Philippians 2:2-11). It seems like from the moment they are born until they reach adulthood, this is a never-ending assignment for parents—helping our children focus on the needs of others.

The high school years (and really even before this) are an excellent opportunity to take this principle from theory to application. As parents, we can focus on having a servant-leader mindset, teaching them to have a heart for the lost and downtrodden. We can help them battle the culture's emphasis on materialism and encourage selflessness and the life of sacrifice to which Christ calls us. One of the most effective strategies for taking this principle from theory (talk, sermons, and chapel messages) to application (actually doing it) is serving through missions. Of course the goal, as I shared earlier in the book, is that by the time your child reaches high school, he has developed a pattern of service and missions. I would highly recommend doing this as a family as much as possible. Many churches offer great opportunities for the youth, but rarely do they pull the entire family together, so you may have to create the opportunity or intentionally include as many family members as possible on a church-related activity.

One of the highlights of my life has been going on mission trips to Cuba with my wife and sons. It is amazing what a short-term mission trip can do for a family. When I returned from my first mission trip to Cuba, I was an emotional wreck. I literally could not even talk about it for several days without crying. I tried to share with Delinda about the wonderful experience, but I could not finish a sentence. I was overwhelmed with emotion because of what had taken place in my heart. My first worship service back at my home church of Prestonwood Baptist Church, I felt like I was an alien observing the people around me. I was convicted of taking the comfort and freedom I enjoyed for granted. I had just attended a service in a Cuban home and the worship music was played on an old cassette tape player. I could not get the picture out of my mind of the Cuban lady lifting her hands in adoration to our Lord—and the tears streaming down her face, as we worshipped in the living room of a home. All four of my boys have had the life-changing experience that traveling to Cuba and ministering to others can provide.

I have witnessed hundreds of high school students returning from our annual mission trips we conduct at our school and church—changed forever. I watched one of our young ladies raise several thousand dollars for Christmas gifts for all of the orphans at the Honduras orphanage where she had spent a week. Not only did she raise the money, she and several of her classmates bought the gifts and shipped them to the children in the orphanage. Then, while most of us were enjoying our Christmas here in the States, she and her mom were with the orphans in Honduras. I have witnessed story after story of high school students dealing face to face with materialism and learning to be grateful for the smallest of things by serving and sacrificing on the mission field. The attitude adjustment that occurs when one is exposed to different cultures is priceless.

Servant-leadership in your community

By now, you know how I feel about going on mission trips. However, if a trip to a foreign country is not possible, your child's community, church, and school can also be an excellent place to serve. Through our school's Student Leadership Institute program, we have hundreds of high school students serving in diverse ways at their school and in their churches. One group of students provides special outreach socials for our school's custodial and cafeteria staff. Another group volunteers on Sunday mornings in the special needs ministry of our church. The same students also volunteer on Friday nights throughout the year so that the parents of the children with special needs can go out on dates. There is also a group that spends time with our sixth grade students, mentoring and investing into their lives. In addition, yet a different group serves on Wednesday nights in our church's children's program, helping with the Bible study and activities. The list goes on and on. Ministry and service projects provide opportunities for incredible growth as we try to develop the proper attitude of servant-leadership.

The worldview issue—building on the foundation already set

The second area during your four-year high school plan is the depth of the Christian worldview of your son or daughter. Several times throughout this book, I have referred to the area of worldview development. There has been a growing concern from church leaders that students are not receiving sufficient biblical worldview training, and research supports this. Astin's (2005) research at UCLA and Christian Smith's (2005) work suggest a concern that because of the lack of biblical worldview training, students are entering college with a weak foundation. Our kids are entering college with a religious pluralistic worldview, characterized by an erosion of belief in the existence of objective biblical truth. A very high percentage of Christian students reflect ambivalence and confusion regarding core doctrine and worldview principles.

Our children can and should be better prepared for the worldview clashes that can cripple their faith. I believe there is good news mixed within this trend. In fact, my own doctorate dissertation project focused on whether or not intentional biblical worldview training made a difference, and it does. Plenty of research studies conclude our students can improve in this area. It is no secret that there is a growing hostility toward Christian beliefs, but be encouraged that specific worldview beliefs and confidence can be increased. Salvation and thinking Christianly are two different concepts. Yes, the first step toward discipling your child is for the child to profess Christ as his or her Lord. But the second step of fulfilling the Great Commission (Matthew 28:19-20) is to teach and train our children—to understand the whole story of God's Word, including the call to be holy and Christlike. The ultimate goal for our children should be for them to think and act like Christ.

Okay, then what is the solution for the biblical worldview problem? I don't think this question is difficult to answer—spend more time intentionally training in the area of Christian worldview. But for some reason—denial, ignorance, or a lack of courage—most of our leaders at seminaries, churches, schools, and in the home are asleep at the wheel. We keep using the same training model over and over again. We seem to be insane in our training: doing the same thing but expecting different results. Too many parents have abdicated their responsibility to the church and to other entities. This may sound sacrilegious, but I believe that many churches have actually convinced parents that they (the church) are the experts and the epicenter of training. Slowly, the parents have decreased their training role and have turned it over to the church.

I will never forget debating a youth pastor who was livid that a parent had decided to send his son to a summer worldview training program instead of the church youth camp. When the youth pastor took his first breath I asked, "Please show me in the Bible where you, instead of the parents, are in charge of the discipleship decisions for that student? And, furthermore, you should be applauding this parent and thanking him for taking his son's spiritual development more seriously."

Don't get me wrong, I am a churchman, and in no way would I ever want to dishonor the God-ordained institution—the church. But the church is not responsible for discipling my children. The ministries of the church have not been assigned to mentor, disciple, and train my children—they are to assist me, the parent. And the same is true for Christian schools; they should only be in partnership with the parents, assisting them in the training of their children.

It is not fair to place this responsibility on churches or any other entity. How can a youth minister who spends one to two hours a week at most with my children successfully fulfill the worldview training? Our expectations are too high. Need I cite any more research that clearly points out that the training model we have used the past thirty or forty years simply is not adequate? The only difference in most church training programs today from the past is that now there is better technology. What I expect out of the church is weekly worship, Bible study, and community—the incredible blessing of being a part of a local body of believers. I want my children to be encouraged by this body of believers and to experience the incredible network of like-minded people. I want the church to assist me in the discipleship process along the way and to be an integral component in creating synergy between home and church around a common belief system. I want my boys to develop friends and a peer network from this body of believers who can encourage and spur them on in the development of their faith. With this said, the church, and all of its wonderful programs, is not meant to replace the parents as the head coaches of their families.

I mentioned earlier that one of the most strategic ministries today at worldview training is Summit Ministries. Several years ago, I opened a piece of mail at the office and pulled out the Summit Ministries Adult Conference brochure. I was instantly intrigued by their philosophy and training model. A few months later, I was in Colorado at the conference. For five straight days, I was systematically presented the most comprehensive and coherent training on the world's dominant worldviews; one of which was, of course, the biblical Christian worldview. They actually developed a matrix with several key disciplines such as biology, law, economics, religion (God), arts, and several others and what each of the four worldviews believed for each one. This is when I realized what was missing from my own training, the curriculum at my school, and my home with my children.

This is also when I started catching the vision for what I now call an Acts 17 disciple. Our children are growing up in a world similar to the Athenian culture Paul was exposed to on a daily basis—a pluralistic society that believed in many gods rather than the one true God. In Acts 17, Paul effectively dealt with the different worldviews. Notice that Paul did not retreat and run back to the church; he did not fall prey to their empty philosophy; he did not charge in and share about Jesus immediately; instead, Paul started talking to the group, and through dialogue and persuasive talk, he gained respect. Through this dialogue, Paul eventually was able to share the gospel and it is recorded that some men believed.

Acts 17 is a great picture of today's university—pluralistic and secular. And, like the apostle Paul, we want our children to enter this environment confident in what they believe and knowledgable of what others believe. Not only do we want to keep them from falling prey to empty deceit and walking away from their faith, we want to equip them to give a cup of living water to their peers and professors. We want to help them share the love of Jesus Christ.

One of my former students from Prestonwood Christian Academy graduated from Princeton University. She had the privilege of taking Dr. Singer's ethics class one semester. Have you ever heard of Dr. Singer? He happens to be one of the most influential voices in mainstream academia in the area of ethics, especially bioethics and the sanctity of life. It does not take long to figure out his radical worldview positions, especially dealing with the sanctity of life. One day she approached Dr. Singer after class and respectfully pointed out that his ethical position on life seemed to differ when it was applied to his circumstances. The young lady had read an article about Dr. Singer's mother who was dying in a hospital. They had good dialogue on this issue and particularly on the apparent inconsistency of his position. Nothing earth shattering happened that day; Dr. Singer did not convert to Christianity nor change his position. But what thrilled me was that my former student was developing into an Acts 17 disciple. In the midst of one of the most liberal universities in the world and in the classroom with arguably the most liberal professor, she did not retreat. She stepped forward. We need Christians to step forward in difficult arenas!

Back to Summit. For this reason, the four-year high school plan for our children includes a Student Conference at Summit Ministries. This two-week conference is the premier worldview training conference for high school students, specifically for those preparing to enter the university. I would highly recommend a focused worldview training time even if this does not particularly excite your child. This conference is not a Disney World trip. In my opinion, if your child has never experienced formal worldview training at church or school (the majority of students have never gone through any training at school), this is a must. I think it is essential even for our children who have been schooled with a focused worldview and Bible curriculum. Indeed, the development of one's worldview is important, but it does not complete a Christian. I agree with Dr. Al Mohler, president of Southern Seminary, who points out that helping students develop a Christian worldview must be balanced with helping the students live out their faith.

Church commitment and small group relationships make a difference before leaving for college. The third area of the four-year high school plan is your child's commitment to church. Church youth ministries matter, but according to the research, not just any youth ministry makes a difference. There are typically three factors within the context of youth ministry that foster spiritual maturity in adolescents: relationships with Christian adults, balanced programming, and the encouragement of spiritual disciplines. The goal is to surround adolescents with a community of caring Christian adults, including parents. Additionally, the peer relationships within the youth group are significant and prove to be a strong correlation between the sense of belonging and being active in the youth ministry. Therefore, during the high school season, it is important to monitor your child's commitment to the youth ministry. Again, your goal and mindset should not just be on high school, rather on the post-high school phase when your child will be at the university.

Closing comments on the high school plan

Focus Areas during High School = Attitude + Worldview Depth + Church Commitment

In addition to elevating my attention to my child's attitude, worldview depth, and church involvement, it is important to consider the necessary life practices discussed in Chapter Five. There were two specific areas defined by lifelong practices that we desired for our children in order to continue their spiritual journey on their own. The spiritual disciplines include personal prayer, Bible study, Scripture memory, active participation in a vibrant church, accountability and mentoring relationships, and a commitment to missions and service. The biblical principles of adulthood include family, work, church, stewardship (finances, tithing, giving), and a vision for manhood/womanhood.

I mention the necessary life practices because of the unique season of maturity our children go through from age sixteen to eighteen. We certainly want our children, especially by their senior year of high school, to begin consistently practicing the spiritual disciplines before they leave our home. Of course, accountability can still be provided when our children go off to the university but it understandably changes when we cannot observe them on a daily basis. The necessary life practices are the areas that you have established as core values for your family. All of them are important, but some of them are more practical in nature.

For example, work ethic was very important to us. We wanted to make sure our children had a job for at least two years before they went away to college. Making money was secondary to all of the other life lessons they would learn while working. Managing their money and appreciating the dollar, so to speak, were important. One other thing that we felt was very beneficial for their university preparation was actually taking some college courses. Usually the summer between the junior and senior year, our sons would go to college. We tried to honor each child's bent by providing a college experience they would be interested in. Bryce and Luke attended the Yale summer sessions and took two classes. Zeke, however, did a three-week internship at Florida State University's Film School because of his interest in film production.

Our goal was twofold. First, we wanted to expose them to the college life a year early to use the experience as a practice session. Our daily talks on the phone were always lively due to the different environment they were in. A year later when they went off to college, it was not as difficult because they already had a taste for it. And it was not as tough on Mom and Dad either—it really helped prepare us for the emotional fall of having one less son around the dinner table. The second reason we did this was simply for them to have to live on their own for a few weeks. They had to wash their own clothes, take care of their meals, and get up on their own. I know this sounds elementary, but I really wanted them to have a short "practice run" of college before the real college experience took place. I think my boys entered college pretty confident and less apprehensive. This may not sound very spiritual, but I would suggest that often it is the everyday life experiences that seem to overwhelm our children as they mature into adulthood. The bottom line is that spiritual maturity does not take place in a vacuum. It takes place when our children have to get themselves out of bed, wash their own clothes, and deal with roommates that might not be of kindred spirit.

I have dropped three of my four sons off at the university and have walked with thousands of other parents who have done the same. I hope you are encouraged when I state that I have never quite felt 100 percent confident that my children were ready (nor have I sensed this from other parents). Indeed, I wish I would have better prepared them or talked to them more. Something tells me that even Jesus felt this way on the eve of Graduation of His academy. Just hours before He was to begin His march to the cross, He was washing the feet of His disciples. He was squeezing in one more important lesson. Don't feel discouraged, parents, if you get to this point and you want to squeeze in one more discussion. It is natural.

Sending our children to the university, military, trade school, or workforce after 6,570 days of practice (birth to diploma) is just not an easy thing to do. However, I can assure you that if you have been purposeful in your parenting, your child will be ready to run with the horses. The next 1,500 days (four years of college) of their life will be a transitional period. Parenting certainly does not end during this time. In fact, some of the most important decisions and discussions will take place during these four years. It is simply a new stage in parenting . . . not over, just different.

This chapter has dealt with three primary areas—attitude, worldview depth, and church commitment. I also suggested using the four high school years to continue working through the *TRAINing* objectives, especially the **N**ecessary life practices. There is one more thing that I consider to be of utmost importance: the relationship you have with your child. The high school years often are full of very challenging situations with our children as they mature and become more independent. Establishing your home as a safe place is critical. Regardless of what happens to your children as they begin their post high school pilgrimage, they need to sense that you and your home are always open to them. Our children will experience some of the lowest of lows during their university years, and your unconditional love for them could be exactly what they need to help them through the difficult times.

Chapter 9 Application

1. Worldview depth, attitude, and church commitment are the three key areas during a child's four years of high school. List some practical ways to deal with all of these areas before he/she enters the university. Share with your spouse or a friend.

2. How is your attitude as a parent or leader of children/ youth? Do you model a life of faith and confidence? Are you preparing your child to face the giants with confidence?

3. What are some specific ideas for activities that can be used to instill humility and servant-leadership in your child?

4. Are you carefully analyzing the training plan for the next generation for your church, your child's school or any para-church ministry in which your child is involved? Are you taking steps to fill in any gaps, and how do you plan to do so?

Final Comments

In his book, *The Body*, Chuck Colson states, "Since a biblical worldview involves all of life, the church must equip its members for all of life. Like the military, this begins with the basics and moves on to building the mature character of the seasoned warrior" (Colson, 1992). It is within the context of equipping our children with the basic principles of a biblical worldview that intentional training is grounded. Although we have covered a lot of ground in this book, I want to remind you of some key points I made earlier, especially the danger of making parenting too complicated. As Colson points out, begin with the basics and build from there.

A seasoned warrior, as Colson coined it, is a child who has been through hundreds and thousands of small practice sessions—conversations, prayers, discipline moments, trials, Bible studies, and encouragement. God's Word is the foundational source that should be the focus. Regular discussions around biblical truth not only point our children toward absolute truth, they also define what is important to you—their ultimate role model. And your child's community is another source from which discussions on biblical truth are provided—that is, if this community is like-minded with you. Some of the most important decisions parents make involve the environments to which they entrust their children—school, church, and peer group.

There is indeed a race, but there is no doubt in my mind that parents can disciple their children to thrive in the thickets—children who revere God and surrender to His transcendent purpose, children who are discerning and who have direction, children who develop deep resolve and inner strength due to dealing with trials and tribulations, and who grow into men and women who follow God, are involved in His church, and who carry on the faith and traditions to your grandchildren. It can be done. It must be done. Training children to "run with the horses" is no easy task, but it is possible.

"I can do all things through Christ who strengthens me." (Philippians 4:13 NKJV)

Appendix
Parent Resources

Most of these resources (compiled by PCA's Biblical worldview director, Mr. Dan Panetti) can be found on Prestonwood Christian Academy's website (prestonwoodchristian.org). The word resource comes from a Latin concept that means "to rise up"—and that is exactly what these resources are intended to do. I hope that you will find these books and articles encouraging and that they will help equip you on your own personal journey with Jesus. My desire is to build up the body of Christ—strengthen, equip, empower!

These resources are categorized into five areas for spiritual development. Similar to a well-balanced meal, a sampling from each of these five areas helps you grow and mature in your walk in a holistic manner. Not only will you grow in your understanding of God's Word, but also in how these biblical principles and truths apply to the world around us—including how we raise our children and strengthen our marriages!

I hope this will assist you in developing your Kingdom Family Plan. In addition to the suggested reading material, I want to encourage you to also consider several conference-based training opportunities such as:

- **Probe Ministry**—They offer a website that provides scholarly and practical information for most major worldview topics. Probe scholars have studied, synthesized, and written brief papers on many current cultural issues. They are an excellent resource to assist you in strengthening your biblical worldview foundation.

- **Summit Ministries**—A ministry I mentioned several times in the book. It provides student and adult training conferences as well as reading material. I consider Summit the number one training ministry on worldview and critical thinking development for all ages. Visit their website for more information.

- **Mission Trips**—The first category below is Passion and Devotion. My highest recommendation for personal growth in this area is to go on a mission trip and to eventually take your family. Reading about this topic is fine but it is only theory; being a "doer of the Word" (James 1:22) is about going and practicing your faith . . . the world becomes your classroom.

- **Sky Ranch Family Camps**—One of the nation's largest camp ministries for youth also conducts family camps. They have weeklong family camps nestled in the beautiful Rocky Mountains of Colorado at their Ute Trail campus. Our family has grown closer to the Lord and to each other at this camp. They have first class facilities, great staff, fun outdoor activities and daily training on parenting and family development.

- **Student Leadership University (SLU)**—Dr. Jay Strack, one of the most influential leaders of this generation, started this leadership organization. SLU partners with local churches, schools and families to give teenagers and executive level leadership training through the lens that leadership begins at the feet of Jesus. Over four cumulative experiences take students behind the scenes of Orlando, San Antonio, Washington, D.C., Europe and the Holy Land to learn the essence of leadership. All four of the Taylor boys have attended SLU and been trained by this unique ministry.

The Five Areas for Spiritual Development:

One: Passion and Devotion:

He therefore is the devout man, who lives no longer to his own will, or the way and spirit of the world, but to the sole will of God.
—William Law, *A Serious Call to a Devout and Holy Life*

Moral character is assessed not by what a man knows but by what he loves.

—St. Augustine

The concept of passion, zeal, and devotion as part of the Christian walk has unfortunately been distorted by a few. While other religious factions promote zeal without knowledge, the Bible warns against this (Proverbs 19:2) and encourages the Christian to walk in truth while living passionately for the Lord. Great men and women of the faith now surround us as a cloud of witnesses encouraging us with their testimonies to throw off the sin that so easily entangles and run with perseverance the race marked out for us (Hebrews 12:1-2). As Isaac Ambrose wrote in *The Christian Soldier:* "Soldiers of Christ . . . you have an arduous work allotted to you, and . . . you have neither time nor talent to throw away." Let us live a life of devotion and passion to the glory of God and walk in a manner worthy of our calling (Ephesians 4:1).

TITLE:	AUTHOR:
Don't Waste Your Life	John Piper
A Serious Call to a Devout and Holy Life	William Law
Serious Times: Making Your Life Matter in an Urgent Day	James Emery White
Thoughts for Young Men	J.C. Ryle

Hard to Believe: The High Cost and Infinite Value of Following Jesus	John MacArthur
The Cost of Discipleship	Dietrich Bonhoeffer
The Roots of Endurance: Invincible Perseverance . . .	John Piper
Contending for Our All: Defending Truth and Treasuring Christ . . .	John Piper
Roaring Lambs: A Gentle Plan to Radically Change Your World	Bob Briner
Teaching to Change Lives: Seven Proven Ways . . .	Howard Hendricks
Defending the Faith: J. Gresham Machen . . .	D.G. Hart

Two: Biblical Literacy:

I *have hidden your word in my heart that I might not sin against you.*

−Psalm 119:11

For Ezra had devoted himself to the study and observance of the Law of the Lord, and to teaching its decrees and laws in Israel.

−Ezra 7:10

Even the Great Commission commands us to teach others all that God has commanded (Matthew 28:20). Implicit in that commandment is that we must know God personally and know His Word intimately and thoroughly. God encouraged the Israelites to impress His commandments on their children and to talk about His Word throughout the entire day (Deuteronomy 6:7-9). We are encouraged to correctly handle the Word of God (2 Timothy 2:15), which is useful for teaching, rebuking, correcting, and training in righteousness so that we may be equipped for every good work (2 Timothy 3:16-17).

God's Word is flawless (Proverbs 30:5) and valuable not only for "religious" issues such as salvation, but also as the primary basis upon which we make other life decisions including decisions about work, family, wealth, health, ministry, and our relationships with others.

Laying the Groundwork

TITLE:	AUTHOR:
30 Days to Understanding the Bible	Max Anders
The Case for Christ (. . . for Faith . . . for a Creator)	Lee Strobel
Christian Beliefs: Twenty Basics Every Christian Should Know	Wayne A. Grudem
Why I Am a Christian	John Stott
Christianity—A Follower's Guide	Pete Briscoe, Editor

Journey to Maturity

TITLE:	AUTHOR:
Basic Christianity	John Stott
Knowing God	J.I. Packer
Mere Christianity	C.S. Lewis
The Pilgrim's Progress	John Bunyan
The Pursuit of God	A.W. Tozer
131 Christians Everyone Should Know	Christian History Magazine
The Normal Christian Life	Watchman Nee
The Mark of a Christian	Francis Schaeffer
Sit Walk Stand	Watchman Nee
Know What You Believe: Connecting Faith and Truth	Paul Little
Pursuit of Holiness	Jerry Bridges
Faith That Goes the Distance	Jud Wilhite
What's So Amazing About Grace?	Phillip Yancey

Kingdom Education: God's Plan for Educating Future Generations	Dr. Glen Schultz
The Question of God: C.S. Lewis and Sigmund Freud Debate God . . .	Armand M. Nicholi, Jr.
Indelible Ink: 22 Prominent Christian Leaders Discuss . . . Their Faith	Scott Larsen, Editor
The Search for Satisfaction: Looking for Something New Under the Sun	Dr. David McKinley
The Seven Checkpoints: Seven Principles Every Teenager Needs to Know	Andy Stanley

Learning to Read & Study Your Bible

TITLE:	AUTHOR:
What the Bible is All About: Bible Handbook: NIV Edition	Henrietta C. Mears
How to Pray and How to Study the Bible	R.A. Torrey
The Big Picture: Understanding the Story of the Bible	Tommy Nelson
How to Study the Bible: Practical Advice for Receiving Light from God's Word	Watchman Nee
Living by the Book	Howard Hendricks

Going Deeper

TITLE:	AUTHOR:
The Call: Finding and Fulfilling the Central Purpose of Your Life	Os Guinness
Spiritual Leadership: Principles of Excellence for Every Believer	J. Oswald Sanders
Essentials of Evangelical Theology, Volumes 1 & 2	Donald Bloesch
The Cost of Discipleship	Dietrich Bonhoeffer
Systematic Theology	Wayne Grudem
Orthodoxy	G.K. Chesterton

A Life Well Spent	Russ Crosson
How We Got the Bible	Neil R. Lightfoot
Embracing the Mysterious God: Loving the God We Don't Understand	James Emery White
A Search for the Spiritual: Exploring Real Christianity	James Emery White
The Doctrines that Divide: A Fresh Look at the Historical Doctrines . . .	Erwin Lutzer

Devotionals

TITLE:	**AUTHOR:**
My Utmost for His Highest	Oswald Chambers
One-Year Book of Devotions for Men	Stuart Briscoe
The Women of Faith Daily Devotional	Patsy Clairmont
Renewed Day by Day	A.W. Tozer
Daily Grace for Teens: Devotional Reflections to Nourish Your Soul	John Maxwell
Teach Me to Pray: 365 Readings	Andrew Murray
Devotional Classics: Selected Readings for Individuals and Groups	Editor: Richard Foster
Morning & Evening	Charles H. Spurgeon

Three: Spiritual Disciplines:

But his delight is in the law of the Lord, and on his law he meditates day and night.

—Psalm 1:2

In the morning, O Lord, you hear my voice; in the morning I lay my requests before you and wait in expectation.

—Psalm 5:3

Prayer, fasting, meditation, memorization, solitude, service, worship, and study are just some of the essential ingredients to be practiced by believers as part of the maturing and growing Christian "walk." Each area can be strengthened, broadened, and fortified to create a deeper knowledge and love for the Lord, resulting in a balanced Christian life. Weaknesses should be strengthened, and strengths should be continuously surrendered to the Lord lest we become prideful. We are not to worship the disciplines themselves, but practicing spiritual disciplines places us in a position to experience the presence and work of the Lord in our lives.

TITLE:	AUTHOR:
Celebration of Discipline: The Path to Spiritual Growth	Richard Foster
The Spirit of the Disciplines: Understanding How God Changes Lives	Dallas Willard
The Complete Works of E.M. Bounds on Prayer	E.M. Bounds
Spiritual Disciplines for the Christian Life	Donald S. Whitney
Lord, Teach Me to Pray in 28 Days	Kay Arthur
Praying God's Word	Beth Moore
How to Develop a Powerful Prayer Life	Dr. Gregory Frizzell
How to Pray and Study the Bible	R.A. Torrey
How to Study the Bible: Practical Advice for Receiving Light from God's Word	Watchman Nee
Living by the Book	Howard Hendricks

Four: Cultural Apologetics:

Christianity is not a series of truths in the plural, but rather Truth spelled with a capital "T." It is Truth about total reality, not just about religious things. Biblical Christianity is Truth concerning total reality—and the intellectual holding of that total Truth and then living in the light of that Truth.

—Francis Schaeffer,
Address at the University of Notre Dame, April 1981.

As Christians, we are called to represent God in the marketplace of ideas, literally to tear down those false arguments and pretensions that set themselves up against the knowledge of God (2 Corinthians 10:5). We should not back down from controversial or difficult discussions and issues of the day; rather, we should speak the truth in love bringing to bear God's Truth revealed in Scripture and written on the hearts of man (Romans 2:15). The love of God should be seen as relevant to the perceived problems of the world—hunger, disease, poverty, crime, etc.—just as Christ called His disciples to feed the hungry and cloth the naked. We must not allow the world or the church to mistakenly spread the "sacred/secular" myth that religion should be separate from reason or that faith is incompatible with facts. We must be wise in dealing with outsiders knowing how to answer everyone (Colossians 4:6). As citizens of two kingdoms, it is our citizenship in the heavenly kingdom that compels us to serve as agents of God's common grace for our temporal kingdom here on earth.

Awakening

TITLE:	AUTHOR:
Serious Times: Making Your Life Matter in an Urgent Day	James Emery White
The Great Experiment: Faith and Freedom in America	Os Guinness
The Abolition of Man	C.S. Lewis
Do Fish Know They're Wet: Living in Your World—Without Getting Hooked	Tom Neven

Amusing Ourselves to Death	Neil Postman
The God Who Is There	Francis Schaeffer
How to Be Your Own Selfish Pig: And Other Ways You've Been Brainwashed	Susan S. Macaulay
The Universe Next Door: A Basic Worldview Catalog	James Sire

Awareness

TITLE:	AUTHOR:
Total Truth: Liberating Christianity from Its Cultural Captivity	Nancy Pearcey
How Now Shall We Live?	Chuck Colson
Worldproofing Your Kids: Helping Moms Prepare Their Kids . . .	Lael F. Arrington
Did Man Just Happen? A Pointed Answer for Evolutionists	Dr. W.A. Criswell
Fit Bodies, Fat Minds: Why Evangelicals Don't Think . . .	Os Guinness
Relativism: Feet Firmly Planted in Mid-Air	Francis J. Beckwith
Think Biblically! Recovering a Biblical Worldview	John MacArthur
The Opening of the Christian Mind: Taking Every Thought Captive to Christ	David W. Gill

Action

TITLE:	AUTHOR:
A Christian Manifesto	Francis Schaeffer
Kingdom Education: God's Plan for Educating Future Generations	Dr. Glen Schultz
Practical View of Christianity	William Wilberforce
Has Democracy Had Its Day?	Carl F.H. Henry

Leadership

TITLE:	AUTHOR:
Transforming Leadership: Jesus' Way of Creating Vision . . .	Leighton Ford
Spiritual Leadership: Principles of Excellence for Every Believer	J. Oswald Sanders
Spiritual Leadership Moving People on to God's Agenda	Henry Blackaby

Five: Parenting and Family:

A man ought to live so that everybody knows he is a Christian . . . and most of all, his family ought to know.

—D.L. Moody

The family is the cornerstone of our society. More than any other force it shapes the attitude, the hopes, the ambitions, and the values of the child. And when the family collapses it is the children that are usually damaged. When it happens on a massive scale the community itself is crippled.

—President Lyndon Johnson

From the beginning of the story of man, God demonstrates man's need for intimate relationships with Him and with others. In Genesis 2:24 God establishes the institution of marriage and creates the entity of the family. God's ideal for the family has been under constant attack from that time until today, and Christians must continue to exalt and demonstrate God's design for the foundational relationships and importance of the family. Scripture speaks to the importance of marriage (1 Corinthians 7) as well as the responsibilities of the husband and wife (Ephesians 5:22-33). The Bible gives parents (not the state or the school) authority and responsibility over their children, who are gifts from the Lord (Psalm 127:3-5). Parents are commanded to teach their children the Word of God (Deuteronomy 6:7-9) and to pass on to the next generation their spiritual legacy (Psalm 78). Parents are also encouraged to model Christlike sacrificial love for their children and are to train their children (Proverbs 22:6) and discipline them in fear and admiration of the Lord.

Creating a Christian Home

TITLE:	AUTHOR:
The Most Important Place on Earth: What a Christian Home Looks Like . . .	Robert Wolgemuth
A Life Well Spent	Russ Crosson
52 Family Time Ideas: Draw Closer to Your Kids as You Draw Closer to God	Tim Smith
The Epidemic: The Rot of American Culture . . .	Robert Shaw, M.D.
The Suburban Christian: Finding Spiritual Vitality in the Land of Plenty	Albert Y. Hsu

Discipling Your Children

TITLE:	AUTHOR:
Age of Opportunity: A Biblical Guide to Parenting Teens	Paul David Tripp
Thoughts for Young Men	J.C. Ryle
Parents' Guide to the Spiritual Growth of Children . . .	John Trent, PhD
Parents' Guide to the Spiritual Mentoring of Teens . . .	Joe White
Child Training Tips: What I Wish I Knew When My Children Were Young	Reb Bradley

Teach Them Diligently: How to Use the Scriptures in Child Training	Lou Priolo
Ready for Responsibility: How to Equip Your Children for Work and Marriage	Dr. Bob Barnes
Who's In Charge Here: Overcoming Power Struggles with Your Kids	Dr. Bob Barnes
The Danger of Raising Nice Kids: Preparing Our Children . . .	Timothy Smith
Parenting with Scripture: A Topical Guide for Teachable Moments	Kara Durbin
Raising Confident Kids	Dr. Bob Barnes
Shepherding a Child's Heart	Tedd Tripp

Challenges to Dads

TITLE:	AUTHOR:
A Man of God: Essential Priorities for Every Man's Life	Dr. Jack Graham
Raising a Modern-Day Knight: A Father's Role in Guiding His Son . . .	Robert Lewis
Bringing up Boys: Practical Advice and Encouragement . . .	Dr. James Dobson
Lessons from a Father to His Son	John Ashcroft
Anchor Man: How a Father Can Anchor His Family in Christ . . .	Steve Farrar
Finishing Strong: How Can a Man Go the Distance	Steve Farrar
She Calls Me Daddy: Seven Things Every Man Needs to Know . . .	Robert Wolgemuth
The Complete Gentlemen: A Modern Man's Guide to Chivalry	Brad Miner
The Power of a Praying Husband	Stormie Omartian
The Complete Husband	Lou Priolo

The Exemplary Husband: A Biblical Perspective	Stuart Scott
Renaissance Fathers: Raising Noble Sons	Rick Johnson
Letters from Dad: Unlock the Secret to Leaving a Lasting Legacy . . .	Greg Vaughn
Men Under Construction: Building a Life That Honors God	Dr. Bob Barnes
Fathers and Sons: 10 Life Principles to Make Your Relationship Stronger	Ron and Matt Jenson
Disciplines of a Godly Man	R. Kent Hughes
Better Dads, Stronger Sons: How Fathers Can Guide Boys . . . Rick	Rick Johnson

Encouragement for Moms
TITLE: AUTHOR:

The Power of a Positive Mom	Karol Ladd
Being A Great Mom, Raising Great Kids	Sharon Jaynes
Creative Correction: Extraordinary Ideas for Everyday Discipline	Lisa Whelchel
The Excellent Wife: A Biblical Perspective	Martha Peace
On the Other Side of the Garden: Biblical Womanhood for Today's Woman	Virginia Fugate
The Power of a Praying Wife (and Parent)	Stormie Omartian
The Christian Mom's Idea Book	Ellen Banks Elwell
That's My Son: How Moms Can Influence Boys to Become Men of Character	Rick Johnson
Don't Make Me Count to Three: A Mom's Look at Heart-Oriented Discipline	Ginger Plowman
Wise Words for Moms	Ginger Plowman
Twelve Extraordinary Women: How God Shaped Women of the Bible, and What He Wants To Do with You	John MacArthur

Challenge for Grandparents

TITLE:	AUTHOR:
101 Ways to Love Your Grandkids: Sharing Your Life and God's Love	Dr. Bob Barnes

Dealing with Divorce

TITLE:	AUTHOR:
Between Two Worlds: The Inner Lives of Children of Divorce	Elizabeth Marquardt
Winning the Heart of Your Stepchild	Dr. Bob Barnes

Preparing Them for College

TITLE:	AUTHOR:
College Bound: What Christian Parents Need to Know About Helping Their Kids Choose a College	Thomas A. Shaw
University of Destruction: Your Game Plan for Spiritual Victory on Campus	David Wheaton
How to Stay Christian in College	J. Budziszewski
A Student's Guide to the Core Curriculum	Mark Henrie